DISABILITY LAW FOR
PROPERTY,
LAND USE,
AND ZONING
LAWYERS

D1300066

ROBIN PAUL MALLOY

AMERICAN**BAR**ASSOCIATION

State and Local

Cover design by Kelly Book/ABA Design

Printed in the United States of America.

24 23 22 21 20   5 4 3 2 1

Library of Congress Cataloging-in-Publication Data
Names: Malloy, Robin Paul, 1956– author. | American Bar Association.
  Section of State and Local Government Law, sponsoring body.
Title: Disability law for property, land use, and zoning lawyers / Robin Paul Malloy.
Description: Chicago : American Bar Association, 2020. | Includes bibliographical
  references and index. | Summary: "This book is intended to be a guide for understanding
  disability law as it applies to property, land use, and zoning law practice. It is meant
  to provide an introduction and broad overview of land use law and disability.
  It includes key references and an easy to follow set of examples that assist the reader
  in understanding issues of disability law in the context of property, land use, and
  zoning"—Provided by publisher.
Identifiers: LCCN 2020007302 (print) | LCCN 2020007303 (ebook) |
  ISBN 9781641056779 (hardcover) | ISBN 9781641056786 (ebook)
Subjects: LCSH: Barrier-free design—Law and legislation—United States. |
  City planning and redevelopment law—United States. | Land use—Law and legislation—
  United States. | People with disabilities—Legal status, laws, etc.—United States.
Classification: LCC KF5709.3.H35 M35 2020 (print) | LCC KF5709.3.H35 (ebook) |
  DDC 346.7304/5087—dc23
LC record available at https://lccn.loc.gov/2020007302
LC ebook record available at https://lccn.loc.gov/2020007303

Discounts are available for books ordered in bulk. Special consideration is given to state bars, CLE programs, and other bar-related organizations. Inquire at Book Publishing, ABA Publishing, American Bar Association, 321 N. Clark Street, Chicago, Illinois 60654-759 8.

www.shopABA.org

For
Gina, Giovanni,
Cormick, Macklin, and McKinley

Contents

Preface

This book is intended to be a guide for understanding disability law as it applies to property, land use, and zoning law practice. For many people representing or working with local governments, this may be a new area of legal consideration. It is important to do property development, land planning, and zoning with proper concern for the ability of all people to safely and easily navigate our built environment, including people with disabilities and people seeking to age in place.

Moreover, we must appreciate that disability laws and regulations apply to a wide range of local government activities and services. This includes planning, zoning, and all programs, services, and activities of local government, as well as the building and alteration of certain facilities and structures. Up until now, there has been little guidance on disability law and its application to property, planning, and zoning law. This book undertakes the process of sorting through the numerous and varied sources of disability law in order to present the user with a clear and concise guide to the key provisions of disability law applicable to the work of local government and to property, planning, and zoning lawyers. This book is not meant to be an exhaustive and all-inclusive treatise. It is meant to provide an introduction and broad overview of land use law and disability. It includes key references and an easy-to-follow set of examples that assist the reader in understanding issues of disability law in the context of property, land use, and zoning.

Remember that in practice, one will also need to consult state law that may supplement federal law on these topics.

While developing this book, I have had the assistance of several research assistants. I wish to acknowledge and thank them for assisting me with footnotes and proofreading. They are Christopher Baiamonte, Shannon Crane, Jeffrey Fasoldt, Jr., Emily Keable, Dominique Kelly, Sarah K. Spencer, and Maria Zumpano.

Acknowledgments

In putting this book together, I have included materials from prior projects along with new, revised, and updated information. I wish to acknowledge my prior works from which I have borrowed information, and in some cases, text, in arranging this book.

Robin Paul Malloy, LAND USE LAW AND DISABILITY: PLANNING AND ZONING FOR ACCESSIBLE COMMUNITIES (2015). (In particular but not exclusively, notes 9-67, with accompanying text.)

Robin Paul Malloy, LAND USE AND ZONING LAW: PLANNING FOR ACCESSIBLE COMMUNITIES (2018). (Materials informed this writing generally with respect to such topics as variances, standing, and cases related to demonstrating discrimination.)

Robin Paul Malloy, *A Primer on Disability for Land Use and Zoning Law*, 4 JOURNAL OF LAW, PROPERTY, AND SOCIETY 1-43 (2018). (Revised, updated, and greatly expanded for parts of this book. This is from an open-access journal.)

Robin Paul Malloy, Sarah Spencer & Shannon Crane. *Land Use Law and Sidewalk Requirements Under the Americans with Disability Act*, 51 REAL PROPERTY, ESTATE, AND TRUST LAW JOURNAL 403-429 (2017). (The article informed this book where noted, and in particular, notes 146-190, with accompanying text.)

Robin Paul Malloy, *Inclusion by Design: Accessible Housing and Mobility Impairment*, 60 HASTINGS L.J. 699-748 (2009). (An early exploration of the topic.)

All profits from this book go to support the American Bar Association (ABA) State and Local Government Law Section.

About the Author

Robin Paul Malloy is the E.I. White Chair and Distinguished Professor of Law, and a Kauffman Professor of Entrepreneurship and Innovation at Syracuse University College of Law. He is a leading expert on property, real estate transactions, and land use and zoning law. Malloy is the co-author of the leading casebook on real estate transactions and has published 18 books and more than 30 scholarly articles, in addition to numerous book chapters and essays. He is a pioneer in his work on the intersection of land use law and disability law. Malloy's book LAND USE LAW AND DISABILITY: PLANNING AND ZONING FOR ACCESSIBLE COMMUNITIES (Cambridge University Press 2015), and his casebook, LAND USE AND ZONING LAW: PLANNING FOR ACCESSIBLE COMMUNITIES (Carolina Academic Press 2018) are leading books in the field. In addition to writing on topics related to real estate, property, and land use, Malloy has numerous books that address issues in law and market theory.

1

Introduction

Many people fail to appreciate the significance of disability issues in making our communities accessible and inclusive. In large part, this is because most people usually think in terms of the universal icon for disability: a person in a wheelchair. They think of this icon and then think about how few people they see using wheelchairs. In fact, they are correct about wheelchair use, as wheelchairs are used by only 1% of the population. From this, people conclude that making our natural and built environments accessible often requires the expenditure of a lot of time and money to accommodate very few people. The problem is that while only 1% of the population uses a wheelchair, 25% of our population has a disability of some type. More specifically, approximately 20% to 25% of American families have a family member who has a type of disability that limits mobility creating many urban planning issues.[1] This is a large percentage of the population. These statistics become more significant when we realize that, statistically, disability rates increase as a population ages. With the demographic trend in America toward an aging population, we can expect rates of disability to increase over time. In addition, many people experience temporary disabilities in their lifetime. They might break a leg or need to recover from surgery on a shoulder, knee, or hip. Moreover, many people need access to disability services and programs. These people need the availability of group homes, senior housing, drug rehabilitation centers, medical marijuana dispensaries, and counseling clinics. Disputes over the requirement to provide these uses and services in a community and where to locate them have become a source of increased litigation. Tension also rises when people with disabilities request exceptions and variances from the rules and regulations that generally apply to the use of a particular property. Doubt and confusion arise with respect to who is entitled to an exception or variance, and about the method for evaluating a request. All of this means that property, land use, and zoning professionals are finding it necessary to navigate disability law in order to do their work without violating the rights of people with disabilities.

The broader concern goes beyond thinking about compliance with disability law. Accessibility includes thinking about planning for welcoming and inclusive communities, and property, land use, and zoning professionals need to plan for inclusion and accessibility. This requires attention to demographic

---

1. ROBIN PAUL MALLOY, LAND USE LAW AND DISABILITY: PLANNING AND ZONING FOR ACCESSIBLE COMMUNITIES 5 (2015) (hereinafter, "MALLOY"); ROBIN PAUL MALLOY, LAND USE AND ZONING LAW: PLANNING FOR ACCESSIBLE COMMUNITIES 7 (2018).

trends, available resources, infrastructure, and supporting pro-grams and services that can benefit all residents, especially resi-dents with disabilities and ones seeking to safely and easily age in place. In making our communities more inclusive, we must think in terms of making the natural and built environments safe, secure, and convenient for the use and enjoyment of all residents and visitors. Therefore, as part of the planning pro-cess, we should pay careful attention to matters of accessibil-ity and formally engage in accessibility planning to make sure that all aspects of our local programs, services, and activities are fully accessible to everyone, including people with disabili-ties. We might formalize something similar to an environmen-tal impact statement (EIS) and require an accessibility impact report (AIR). An AIR would be designed to evaluate the current state of accessibility in a community and provide a basis for continuously working toward enhanced inclusion and greater integration of accessibility for everyone. In addition, a particu-larized AIR ought to be required for every development project and every significant planning and zoning application. This way the community can consider the impact of the project or appli-cation in terms of its potential effects on the inclusion of people with disabilities and of people seeking to age in place.

To do this effectively, it is important for property, land use, and zoning professionals to have a basic understanding of the key provisions of disability law that most affect the use and devel-opment of real estate. This book provides such an introduction for people familiar with both property law and land regulation (planning and zoning) but who have little experience with dis-ability law. The goal is to present an introduction that facilitates understanding of the intersections among property, land use, and disability law. In general, the legal requirements of primary concern to property, land use, and zoning lawyers are limited such that only a few parts of our expansive federal disability laws are most relevant to the vast majority of planning and zoning matters. This book will guide the reader through these relevant provisions. Although this book addresses a variety of sources of disability law, it focuses on three Acts: (1) the *Americans with Disabilities Act (ADA)* of 1990 and 2008; (2) the *Fair Housing Act (FHA)* of 1968 and Fair Housing Amendments Act (FHAA) of 1988; and (3) Section 504 of the *Rehabilitation Act (RHA)* of 1973 (codified as Section 794 of the Rehabilitation Act of 1978). In addition, design requirements for items such as doorways, parking spaces, curb cuts, and bathrooms are addressed in the guidelines of the United States Access Board (USAB). The USAB is an independent agency of the U.S. government. It develops and maintains design criteria and guidelines for accessibility of our built environment.

2

Planning, Design, and Use

In general, disability law concerns three key functions: land planning, design, and land use.

LAND PLANNING

Land planning should be deliberative and comprehensive in terms of thinking about the needs of the entire community. This includes continuous planning on how to make a community more accessible to people with disabilities. Moreover, planning should focus on sustainability and on developing a community in which people can easily age in place. A community should be safe, secure, and accessible for people of all ages and capabilities. People should not have to move to a new community simply because they age and need a differently designed type of housing. Likewise, children should have fully accessible playgrounds and recreational facilities within easy reach of their homes and schools. To accommodate all people, planning must be integrative. An accessible community has a seamless web of connectivity among all the places and spaces in which life is lived. It is inappropriate to think in terms of an accessible building or an accessible house without thinking about the accessible routes and transportation systems that connect such places. A fully accessible house may nonetheless leave a person lonely and isolated if there is inadequate attention to connecting a home to the places and spaces of civic life, such as work, play, shopping, entertainment, education, and government. In addition, it is not enough for buildings, roads, public spaces, sidewalks, and parks to be planned for accessibility. Planning must also include the steps that will be taken to develop and finance new programs, services, and activities of local government, including ways of improving existing programs and services and upgrading activities, programs, and services that may be below standard.

Accessibility should be a standard and required element in planning as directed by state and local regulations that call for local municipal planning. Just as we plan for needs related to housing, schools, public services, parks, commercial activity, and roads, we need to plan for accessibility. Many communities already plan for sustainability but fail to include accessibility in these plans. Communities should be required to engage in planning that is focused specifically on the need for accessibility and for aging in place.

Local planning must also comply with the requirements articulated in *Olmstead v. L.C.*[2] and "subsequently mandated in federal disability legislation" (Olmstead planning).[3] "Olmstead

---

2. Olmstead v. L.C., 527 U.S. 581 (1999).

3. *See* MALLOY, *supra* note 1, at 238; *see* U.S. Dep't of Justice, *Statement of the Department of Justice on Enforcement of the Integration Mandate of Title II of the Americans with*

planning requires communities to plan for the best ways to deliver services to people with disabilities in settings that enable them to interact with nondisabled people to the fullest extent possible."[4] This requires us to evaluate the accessibility of all aspects of our communities. One example of where this kind of planning is obvious involves sidewalks, which are held to be services under the Americans with Disabilities Act (ADA). As services, communities must plan how to make sidewalks accessible to the fullest extent possible. Moreover, comprehensive plans and sustainability plans should both include specifics regarding efforts to transition to fully accessible sidewalks if current sidewalks are not fully accessible.[5]

As part of a planning process, it may be useful to require accessibility impact reports (AIRs). An AIR would be similar to a health impact assessment (HIA) or environmental impact statement (EIS). Further, an AIR would focus on the way land use regulation and property development affect the accessibility of a community. AIRs should include details with respect to sidewalks and transit systems that should be core components of connectivity across the community. They should focus on the best locations for transit services and for building new sidewalks, including appropriate placing of curb cuts, crosswalks, and transit stops. An AIR should also assess access to buildings, facilities, and parks, while accounting for the ongoing need for repairs and updates.

Disabilities Act and Olmstead v. L.C. (June 22, 2011), http://www.ada.gov/olmstead/q&a
_olmstead.htm#_ftnref9.

4. MALLOY, *supra* note 1, at 238; *Olmstead*, 527 U.S. 581; 28 C.F.R. § 35.130(d) (**2020**); Exec. Order No. 13217, 3 C.F.R. 774 (2002), *reprinted in* 42 U.S.C. § 12131 (2006).

5. *See* MALLOY, *supra* note 1, at 238-39. Olmstead plans must contain specifics and not be merely aspirational. Budget constraints are not necessarily a sufficient defense against implementing an Olmstead plan. 28 C.F.R. § 35.130(b)(ii)(7).

More specifically, as to the example of sidewalks, the ADA requires public entities with more than 50 employees to establish transition plans for sidewalk accessibility.[6] These plans should identify needed sidewalk repairs and upgrades that will bring community sidewalks into ADA compliance. Plans should provide for pedestrian access upgrades to "[s]tate and local government offices and facilities, transportation, places of public accommodation, and employers, followed by walkways serving other areas."[7] Each transition plan should accomplish four tasks:

1. Identify physical obstacles in the public entity's facilities that limit the accessibility of its programs or activities to individuals with disabilities.
2. Describe in detail the methods that will be used to make the facilities accessible.
3. Specify the schedule for taking the steps necessary to upgrade pedestrian access to meet ADA and Section 504 requirements in each year following the transition plan.
4. Indicate the official who is responsible for implementation of the plan.[8]

DESIGN

Design issues are also important to accessibility. In fact, design matters are often the first matters that come to mind when one raises the issue of disability in connection with property

---

6. *See* 28 C.F.R. § 35.150(d)(1) (2015); *see also* Robin Paul Malloy, Sarah Spencer & Shannon Crane, *Land Use Law and Sidewalk Requirements Under the Americans with Disabilities Act*, 51 REAL PROP. TR. & EST. L. J. 403 (2017).

7. *See* 28 C.F.R. § 35.150(d)(2) (2015); *see also* MALLOY, *supra* note 6.

8. 28 C.F.R. § 35.150(d)(3); *see also* MALLOY, *supra* note 6.

development, land planning, and zoning. Design concerns focus on things such as making buildings, sidewalks, transportation systems, housing, and other aspects of the built environment accessible. Much of the professional work in the design area is done by architects and building designers. For most lawyers, design issues are primarily matters of compliance with building and design codes, including standards for accessible and universal design. There are code books and design guidelines available to assist in achieving accessibility compliance. In fact, the United States Access Board (USAB) provides detailed guidelines that cover a vast array of design issues. Unfortunately, there is no government certification system to evidence a property developer's compliance with accessible design guidelines. In this respect, accessibility efforts are different than having electrical work done on a new home, and then having a certified electrician sign off on compliance with the relevant electrical and building code. In the area of accessibility, there are rules of accessibility and design guidelines, but one typically must engage a private consultant or architect for advice on compliance. In this case, the property owner or operator generally remains liable for compliance, but based on their particular engagement contract with a private consultant or architect, the owner or operator may have recourse against their private consultant for failure of compliance.

Beyond specific design issues, such as having wider residential hallways, larger bathrooms, larger handicap parking spaces, and providing curb cuts and ramps, design approaches fall into two general categories. The first category is "visitability." The second category is "universal design." Visitability involves a level of accessibility that makes particular venues, such as a residential home, reasonably accessible in terms of the main social gathering areas of the house. The idea is that a structure should be able to be safely visited by anyone who might come over for a social visit or for a short stay. This would mean that the entranceway, first-floor bathroom, and entertaining areas of the home are readily accessible. Other parts of the house may be not readily accessible by a person with disabilities. This contrasts with the more pervasive approach of universal design. Universal design seeks to make everything universally accessible to people of different abilities. This approach would make accessibility a primary goal throughout the entire structure. It also would seek to make it possible for everyone to be able to use all aspects of the home in a similar way, without regard to their ability.

More particularly, the Department of Justice (DOJ) has established Standards for Accessible Design that apply to state and local government facilities, as well as to places of public accommodation and commercial facilities.[9] As to state and local facilities that were constructed or altered after certain dates, they must be readily accessible and able to be used by people with disabilities in accordance with accessible design standards, unless the state or local government entity can demonstrate that it is "structurally impracticable" to meet the requirements.[10]

---

9. UNITED STATES ACCESS BOARD, ABA STANDARDS, https://www.access-board.gov/guidelines-and-standards/buildings-and-sites/about-the-aba-standards/aba-standards/single-file-version (last visited Oct. 22, 2019) [*hereinafter* ABA STANDARDS]. The standards implement the Architectural Barriers Act (ABA).

10. New construction or work on altered state and local government facilities that began on or after March 15, 2012, must comply with the 2010 ABA STANDARDS. New construction or work on altered state and local government facilities that began on or after September 15, 2010, and before March 15, 2012, must comply with either the 1991 ABA STANDARDS, the Uniform Federal Accessibility Standards (UFAS), or the 2010 ABA STANDARDS. Any new construction or alterations that began before September 15, 2010, must comply with either the 1991 ABA STANDARDS or the UFAS. U.S. DEP'T OF JUSTICE, ADA REQUIREMENTS: EFFECTIVE DATE – COMPLIANCE DATE, https://www.ada.gov/revised_effective_dates-2010.htm (last visited Nov. 13, 2019). New construction is defined as a building that was designed for first occupancy

In general, this requires the state or local entity to demonstrate "unique characteristics" that make accessible design impracticable. An example might be identifying the difficulty of dealing with soil conditions or a difficult terrain to meet accessible design standards.[11]

Federal buildings and facilities are not subject to the same regulations as entities of state and local government. Federal buildings and facilities are subject to the Architectural Barriers Act (ABA).[12] In practice, the ABA standards are similar to the ADA, but they apply to facilities that are designed, built, altered, or leased with certain federal funds. Typical facilities covered include federal buildings, social security offices, post offices, and government-funded public housing. Places of public accommodation also have design standards that are applicable to new construction and to existing buildings and their alteration.

The legal issues related to design involve compliance with government regulations that require accessibility and figuring out the legal meaning of certain terms and standards used in disability law. It is not so much about design as it is about the interpretation of when certain actions, such as updating an existing building, rise to the level of requiring full design compliance with accessibility rules. Property owners and government officials may have a different conception of what meets the standard of accessibility compared to disability rights advocates.

---

beginning January 26, 1993, or later. An altered facility is defined as an existing building that undergoes alterations. 28 C.F.R. § 36.401.

11. 28 C.F.R. § 36.401.

12. The ABA STANDARDS are established by the General Services Administration, the Department of Defense, the Department of Housing and Urban Development, and the United States Postal Service. ABA STANDARDS, *supra* note 9.

Many times, the difference ends up being related to the cost of achieving a certain level of accessibility. Likewise, legal issues center on the claims that can be made by people with disabilities and the defenses that can be offered by defendants.

LAND USE REGULATION

Land use regulation involves the public and private regulation of land use and the coordination of land uses within a community. Zoning is the public regulation of land use and concerns publicly adopted regulations that control and coordinate land uses within a jurisdiction. There are also private regulations governing land use. Private regulations are adopted by and among private property owners and are established in private documents. Examples of documents include covenants and restrictions that regulate land uses in a subdivision and a declaration of condominium, which regulates uses in a condominium project. Private land regulations may also be located in deeds and other documents that create and transfer interests in land. Public zoning regulations are adopted by local governments under the delegated authority of the police power of the state. Zoning regulations must be made pursuant to a comprehensive plan. Zoning regulations are authorized as an exercise of the police power to protect the public health, safety, welfare, and morals. Zoning regulations are enforced by public officials, and public officials are empowered to consider and grant exceptions and variances from the rules based on established criteria. Private land regulations are created by private property owners and enforced by private parties. This becomes a source of confusion when homeowners in a private subdivision seek to have a zoning board enforce compliance with a restrictive covenant that regulates the use of property in their subdivision. Public officials enforce public land regulations; in the case of private land regulations, individuals have to go to their homeowners association board (or equivalent) and then to court to enforce their own private land use restrictions. In both situations, for both public and private land regulation, restrictions may limit the types of permitted uses and things like building height, setbacks, and various housing design and use features of the property and the improvements thereon. Two questions that need to be asked when dealing with disability law and its relationship to property, land use, and zoning, are whether these public and private regulations violate requirements of our disability laws, and whether they result in unlawful discrimination.

Legal questions arise when we try to implement federal law that protects the rights of people with disabilities in the context of potentially conflicting local law arising pursuant to public or private land regulations. Key among these concerns are the requirements related to protecting people with disabilities from discrimination in the function and application of local land regulations and in responding to the requirement of providing a reasonable accommodation or modification in public and private land and housing rules and procedures.

Even though disability law presents significant tension among federal, state, and local law, none of the federal disability laws, including the ADA, the Fair Housing Act (FHA), and the Rehabilitation Act (RHA), preempt local property, land use, and zoning law. Federal disability laws are not planning and zoning laws—they are laws enacted to protect the rights of people with disabilities. Therefore, federal disability laws do not preempt local land use and zoning law, nor do they preempt private land regulations that were created in accordance with state property law. Federal disability laws proscribe discrimination and protect the rights of people with disabilities. These federal acts are applicable to local government planning and zoning and to private land use regulations, but the federal acts do not preempt them. This means that property, land use, and zoning professionals need to understand the relationships among federal disability law, and state and local land law. These laws establish certain duties, obligations, and liabilities for professionals who work in this area.

Before outlining relevant provisions of our disability law, I set out some common examples of issues that arise at the intersection of land use and disability law. For the most part, the examples are about use issues rather than design issues. Design issues related to doorways, curb cuts, accessible bathrooms, and the like are primarily the concern of architects and code enforcers. The more relevant issues for land use and zoning lawyers concern uses and the coordination of uses across a community. The following examples describe scenarios where one might encounter disability law questions in a land use and zoning context. These examples come from real zoning appeals and court cases. All of these examples are problematic, and they all require analysis under our disability law and under traditional land use and zoning laws. This means that all of the following situations require local planning and land use professionals to make special inquiries and findings of fact under disability law. Many of these situations impose risk because the answers are, as of yet, less than clear. The goal of this book is to provide an introduction to the law relevant to resolving the disability issues raised in the situations described.

- A zoning regulation prevents group homes in a specific district or it permits group homes, but provides for special or conditional review only for group homes that serve people with disabilities. Does this difference in treatment under the code result in discrimination against people with disabilities? [*Most likely. There will need to be a rational and important state interest in justifying different treatment for the group home for persons with disabilities. This is because people with disabilities are a protected class.*]

- Planning and zoning regulations require the use of sand for all pathways that lead to the waterfront of a river or lake. The stated purpose of this regulation is to maintain a permeable surface and reduce rainwater runoff problems along the waterfront. This regulation results in a soft surface, which functionally limits access to the waterfront for people with certain mobility impairments and people who use walkers or wheelchairs. As a result, people with a disability are not able to enjoy the waterfront in the same way as people who don't have a disability are able to enjoy it. Even though the requirement for a sandy walkway may meet an environmental objective, it simultaneously results in a negative consequence for people with certain disabilities. [*This policy likely will be subject to a successful challenge. Local officials will need to be able to explain why there are no alternative ways of accomplishing the goal without providing some reasonable access for people with disabilities.*]

- Zoning regulations limit the location of drug rehabilitation centers. A potential drug rehabilitation operator seeks to locate in a zone that does not permit such centers. Should the operator be permitted to operate in the zone, even though the code prohibits operation in this location? What if the operator asserts a right to operate in this zone without regard to the zoning code on the ground that, as an entity that provides services to people who may be considered to have a disability, it is entitled to a reasonable accommodation or modification of the zoning code? Most importantly, what factors must be considered and evaluated in making a decision? [*Under disability law, a person with a disability and certain third parties can sue for a reasonable accommodation/modification. This leaves open the issue of determining the meaning of "reasonable" in this situation. There is a three-factor test, as will be discussed in this book. It must be (1) reasonable, (2) necessary, and (3) it cannot fundamentally alter the program, service, or activity.*]

- A not-for-profit organization seeks to open and operate a boarding house for women who are "struggling with life controlling problems." Life-controlling problems may include emotional stress or depression or the abuse of drugs and alcohol. Under the zoning code, group homes are restricted by a size limit, but this boarding house would seek to have twice as many people living in it than is permitted under the code for a group home. The organization seeks an exception to the zoning code under the laws that protect people with disabilities. Key issues to consider include (1) does the city have to provide an exception to its zoning ordinance; (2) what are the criteria for deciding the matter (e.g., what specific findings must be made when making a decision); (3) are women struggling with "life-controlling issues" within the definition of persons with disabilities; and, (4) what if only some of the women, but not all of the women, who will occupy the boarding house have a recognized disability? Further, does the fact that some women in the group may not be legally considered as having a disability disqualify the organization from protection of our disability laws? Stated differently, does every member of the group have to be a member of the protected class in order for the group or organization to successfully assert a right to a reasonable accommodation or modification? [*Not every member of a group has to meet the definition of having a disability. It is unclear what the percentage needs to be, but it is probably a substantial number. Local planning and zoning officials will need to evaluate the three-factor test when determining whether an accommodation/modification is reasonable.*]

- A zoning setback restriction prohibits the addition of a ramp to the front of a home because it will extend into the required front yard setback. Without this ramp, the only way for a person with a wheelchair to enter this home is by putting in a ramp at a doorway in the back of the house. Does a requirement that the person with a disability enter via the back of the house, when the primary entrance is in the front, violate the ADA? If the homeowner is granted a variance for a ramp in the front of the home, can a zoning board require the ramp to be made out of high-quality materials and require the design to blend in with the house, even if it adds thousands of dollars to the cost of the ramp? Can a zoning board approve the variance for the use of a ramp at the front of the house and require that the ramp be removed once the person needing it is no longer residing in the home? Does granting the exception for the ramp run with the land, like a typical variance? What if there is a requirement to restore the front of the house to its original design after the person leaves the home and this imposes a substantial cost on the homeowner? Do regulations and conditions that impose higher costs or extra burdens on people with a disability violate the ADA, FHA, or RHA? [*The ramp probably needs to be allowed as a reasonable accommodation. Whether it should be located at the front door or at the back of the house will depend on a determination of what is reasonable, including what might be readily achievable in seeking to remove this barrier to accessibility. The design and materials used to build the ramp can also be regulated. This is true even if the regulations impose more costs on the person with a disability relative to some other design and the use of some other materials. As to requiring restoration of the property after the person with a disability moves, this is permitted within limits.*]

- A zoning regulation prohibits horses, alpacas, donkeys, and pigs in single-family residential neighborhoods. A resident living on a one-acre lot has a miniature horse in her yard because it is a service and emotional support animal for her daughter. Neighbors complain about the smell of manure. Is the resident entitled to keep the miniature horse, even though it is not otherwise permitted under the zoning ordinance? [*Maybe. If it is a service animal under the ADA, it is likely permitted, assuming sanitary and safety procedures are in place to prevent the service animal from being a danger to public health, safety, and welfare. On the other hand, if it is an emotional support animal, a zone variance will depend on an evaluation of what constitutes a reasonable accommodation under the circumstances.*]

- A zoning code permits people to operate home offices in their homes. In this community, a number of lawyers and insurance agents have home offices in their single-family, residential homes. Even if the single-family home does not need to meet ADA design guidelines, must it do so to the extent that the home office transforms a part of the house into a place of public accommodation that must be accessible under the ADA? [*Yes. This includes an accessible pathway into the part(s) of the home used for meeting with the public.*]

- A city located in the "snow belt" region of the country refuses to plow the snow from sidewalks during the winter. By not removing the snow after a snowfall, the sidewalks become inaccessible to people with disabilities. A disability rights group sues the city for a violation of the disability laws. The group claims that the sidewalks are a service, program, or activity of the local government, and as such, the sidewalks must be maintained in an accessible manner. The city responds that sidewalks are structures and not a service, program, or activity of local government. The city asserts that disability law does not govern snow removal from city sidewalks. Which position is correct? [*Sidewalks are not only facilities; they may be facilities that receive federal funding. Likewise, sidewalks are considered programs, services, and activities of local government. In each case, sidewalks are covered under our disability laws. The city needs to maintain the accessibility and usability of its sidewalks. This includes snow removal.*]

- A city has an old sidewalk system, much of which does not meet current ADA requirements in its design. The city is currently considering doing some infrastructure work on Main Street. The city is deciding between work that will fill potholes and put fresh sealcoat on the surface of the street, or just redoing the roadway. The city is challenged by some residents to upgrade the sidewalks in the area in order to comply with the new ADA standards. The city claims that the sidewalks are grandfathered in, until and unless the city does new sidewalk construction. This raises a question regarding the need to upgrade sidewalks. The answer turns on the interpretation of the meaning of "altering" the street. While normal street maintenance is not an alteration, going beyond normal maintenance may rise to the level of an alteration and require bringing adjoining sidewalks into compliance with new ADA design requirements. [*New construction and alteration work requires that the sidewalks must be accessible to the fullest extent possible. The only defense is structural impracticability.*]

- A church building located in a city does not have an accessible entrance. Does this violate disability laws or is there an exemption for a religious organization? If the church decides to add a daycare center, does the daycare center need to be accessible because it will be providing a place of public accommodation, or is it exempt? [*There is an exemption for religious organizations, but if they receive federal funds, they are subject to Section 504 of the RHA.*]

- A commercial home builder develops subdivisions of single-family residential homes. In the subdivisions, the developer offers a choice of five different model homes from which consumers may select. While the model home choices have various design options and layouts, none of the homes offer an accessible entrance (all have multiple-step entryways), and none offer a wheelchair-accessible bathroom. A potential home buyer who uses a wheelchair for mobility asks the developer whether any of the homes can be built with a ramp entrance instead of stairs, and whether the first floor bathroom can be enlarged to be wheelchair accessible. Each of these is a request for a reasonable accommodation or modification. The developer responds and says it does not provide such options. The developer states that the potential buyer must purchase the model as designed, and then engage an independent contractor to do after-market modifications to meet any special accessibility needs. Of course, after-market rehabilitation is generally more expensive than making the adjustments with the original construction. Has the developer violated the FHA by not providing a reasonable accommodation or modification to the home buyer? [*Maybe. Single-family homes do not have very many accessibility requirement's but a case can be made that with new construction a builder should offer some accessible options when requested.*]

- A gated community prohibits buses on the private roads in the subdivision. One family living in the gated subdivision has a child with a severe mobility impairment and seeks to have the public school bus pick up their child and drop him off at their house, rather than at the public road outside the gate that is about half a mile away from their house. The parents petition the homeowners association (HOA) for an exception to the rule that prohibits buses in the subdivision as a reasonable accommodation or modification of the rules. The HOA denies the request. Has the HOA violated the FHA by not granting the request? [*Probably, but it will depend on application of the three-factor test for determining if the request is reasonable.*]

- A private subdivision is governed by restrictive covenants and has rules and regulations that prohibit yard fencing. These anti-fencing rules are enforced by the subdivision's HOA. A couple living in the subdivision have an autistic child who often runs out of the yard and into the street. To secure the safety of their child, the couple petitions the HOA for the right to erect yard fencing on the property. They present the HOA board with a doctor's certification of the disability and of the recommendation for a yard fence. They also present the HOA board with a letter from the state authorizing payment for the fence and its installation by the state. The HOA denies the request. Is this a violation of the requirement for a reasonable accommodation or modification under the FHA? Does it make a difference in the evaluation of this question whether the anti-fencing restriction is in the rules and regulations as opposed to the covenants and restrictions? [*This is probably a violation. The fence is likely reasonable but the HOA may put some conditions on how the fence is constructed and the materials to be used to build it. The HOA may also require that the fence be taken down when the child is no longer residing on the property.*]

These are just a few examples of the issues that arise at the intersection of land use regulation law and disability law. Disability issues come up in all kinds of planning, zoning, and land regulation settings. Questions arise with respect to primary uses, conditional and accessory uses, variances, grandfather provisions, takings, and much, much more. Furthermore, in the planning process and in a zoning board of appeal hearing, you may find yourself representing an adjoining property owner who wants to weigh in on a proposed or requested accommodation to permit an exception to a land regulation to allow a group home or a drug rehabilitation facility in a location that otherwise prohibits such uses. In these situations, you will need to submit evidence to the record concerning the factors and criteria required to be addressed in making a disability law determination. Thus, for example, if one opposes an exception to accommodate a drug rehabilitation facility, one would want to challenge the granting of the exception by submitting evidence that granting such an accommodation is unreasonable. A person with a disability is entitled only to a reasonable accommodation. Therefore, one can oppose an exception by showing that the request is unreasonable. To do this, you will need evidence that addresses reasonableness in terms of cost and benefits, necessity in terms of a "but for" test, and whether granting an exception fundamentally alters the land use and zoning plan.

This book provides a framework for understanding how to best approach disability law issues in your land use and zoning practice.

3

Applicable Federal Law

Property, land use, and zoning laws generally are matters of state law and come within the police powers of the states as reserved under the 10th Amendment to the U.S. Constitution. A professional who practices in these areas must be aware of the interplay between state and federal law. Disability law and the rights of people with disabilities are areas of significant importance in this regard. The following federal legislative acts are the primary sources of federal regulation that guide disability law and the rights of people with disabilities:

- *Architectural Barriers Act (ABA) of 1968.*[13] The ABA requires buildings and facilities that are designed,

---

13. Architectural Barriers Act of 1968, Pub. L. No. 90-480, 82 Stat. 718 (codified as amended at 42 U.S.C. §§ 4151-4157 (2006)). Two useful resources that one can consult on this and other regulations related to the Americans with Disabilities Act (ADA) are BUREAU OF NATIONAL AFFAIRS, BNA'S DISABILITY LAW MANUAL (1992) [*hereinafter* BNA] and PETER A. SUSSER & PETER J. PETESCH, DISABILITY DISCRIMINATION AND THE WORKPLACE (2d ed. 2011) [*hereinafter* SUSSER].

constructed, altered, or leased by using certain federal funds after September 1969 to be accessible to and usable by people with disabilities.[14] It addresses construction-based standards of accessibility for new and renovated buildings rather than the services or programs that are provided in such buildings. Private-market construction of single-family housing is not covered by the ABA.[15]

- *Section 504 of the Rehabilitation Act (RHA) of 1973, codified in Section 794 of the U.S.C. as amended by the Rehabilitation Act of 1978.*[16] Section 504 prohibits discrimination based on disability in any *program or activity* that receives federal financial assistance.[17] Reasonable accommodations must be made for employees, and this includes the physical environment.[18] New construction and alterations must be accessible. To the extent that Section 504 applies to housing, it covers housing programs that receive federal funding and does not cover privately funded single-family residential housing.[19] As to planning and zoning, the *reasonable accommodation* requirement under Section 504 is similar to that of the Fair Housing Act (FHA), but Section 504 applies only to programs and activities that receive federal funds. The FHA has a broader application.[20]

---

14. Architectural Barriers Act of 1968; SUSSER, *supra* note 13 at ch. 1 § II(A) (2d ed. 2011). *See* Laura L. Rovner, *Disability, Equality, and Identity*, 55 ALA. L. REV. 10431043-47 (2004).

15. Architectural Barriers Act of 1968; SUSSER, *supra* note 13.

16. 29 U.S.C. § 794 (2006); *see generally* BNA, *supra* note 13 *and* SUSSER, *supra* note 13.

17. 29 U.S.C. § 794 (2006); *see* Rovner, *supra* note 14, *and* Bonnie P. Tucker, *Section 504 of the Rehabilitation Act After Ten Years of Enforcement: The Past and the Future*, 1989 U. ILL. L. REV. 845, 845-51 (1989).

18. *See* MALLOY, *supra* note 1, at 113.

19. *Id.*

20. *See* 29 U.S.C. § 794 (2006); 42 U.S.C. § 3601 (2006).

- *Fair Housing Act (FHA) of 1968 and Fair Housing Amendments Act of 1988.*[21] The FHA prohibits discrimination in housing on the basis of race, color, religion, sex, national origin, familial status, or disability and applies both to private housing and public-supported housing.[22] Activities covered include selling, advertising, leasing, and financing of housing.[23] Zoning can also be covered. The FHA requires owners and zoning officials to make reasonable exceptions to policies and practices to afford people with disabilities an equal opportunity to obtain housing.[24] The focus is on evaluating the meaning of "providing an equal opportunity to obtain" housing.[25] This may require zoning officials to grant a variance or exception to a zoning requirement, if the person with a disability can show that doing so is a reasonable accommodation and that it is necessary for the person to be afforded an equal opportunity to obtain housing.[26] A "but for" test is used, which requires the person seeking the accommodation to demonstrate that, without the variance or exception ("but for the variance or exception"), the person will not have

---

21. Fair Housing Amendments Act of 1988, Pub. L. No. 100-430, 102 Stat. 1619 (codified as amended at 42 U.S.C. § 3601 (2006)) (amending Civil Rights Act of 1968, Pub. L. No. 90-284, Title VIII, 82 Stat. 81 (codified as amended at 42 U.S.C. § 3601 (2006)). *See generally* BNA, *supra* note 13, *and* SUSSER, *supra* note 13.

22. 42 U.S.C. § 3601.

23. *Id.*

24. *Id.*

25. *Id.*; Commemorating the Anniversary of the Fair Housing Act, H.R. Res. 59, 110th Cong. (2008); 134 Cong. Rec. 15,665 (1988); 134 Cong. Rec. 19,871 (1988).

26. *See generally* Forest City Daly Hous., Inc. v. Town of North Hempstead, 175 F.3d 144 (2d Cir. 1999); Innovative Health Sys., Inc. v. City of White Plains, 931 F. Supp. 222 (S.D.N.Y. 1996), *aff'd* 117 F.3d 37 (2d Cir. 1997).

an equal opportunity to obtain housing.[27] The FHA may also require landlords to make reasonable accommodations, such as permitting a guide dog in an apartment when the apartment has a no-pets policy.[28] The FHA may also require a landlord to permit a tenant to make modifications to a structure in order for it to be reasonably accessible, even if the landlord's lease otherwise prohibits structural modifications.[29] The FHA also provides mandates for all new multi-family housing to meet specific inclusive design standards, including guidelines for common areas, entranceways, hallways, light switches, grab bars, spacing to accommodate the use of a wheelchair, and other design elements.[30] The Department of Housing and Urban Development (HUD) and the Department of Justice (DOJ) issue guidance on design and construction requirements.[31] Failure to make multi-family dwellings accessible and in compliance with these guidelines violates the FHA.[32] The regulations include definition criteria for "dwellings" covered by the FHA (e.g., a hotel room

---

27. *See* Lapid-Laurel, LLC v. Zoning Bd. of Adjustment of the Township of Scotch Plains, 284 F.3d 442 (3d Cir. 2002); Smith & Lee Assocs., Inc. v. City of Taylor, Mich., 102 F.3d 781 (6th Cir. 1996); *and* Sharpvisions, Inc. v. Borough of Plum, 475 F. Supp. 2d 514 (W.D. Pa. 2007).

28. 24 C.F.R. § 100.204(b) (2004). *See* Bronk v. Ineichen, 54 F.3d 425 (7th Cir. 1995).

29. 24 C.F.R. § 100.203(c) (2004). *See* SUSSER, *supra* note 13, at § II(F) *and* Bachman v. Swan Harbour Assoc., 653 N.W.2d 415 (Mich. Ct. App. 2002).

30. 42 U.S.C. § 3604(f)(3)(C).

31. U.S. DEP'T OF HOUS. & URBAN DEV. and U.S. DEP'T OF JUSTICE, ACCESSIBILITY (DESIGN AND CONSTRUCTION) REQUIREMENTS FOR COVERED MULTIFAMILY DWELLINGS UNDER THE FAIR HOUSING ACT (2013), https://www.ada.gov/doj_hud_statement.pdf; U.S. DEP'T OF JUSTICE, 2010 ADA STANDARDS FOR ACCESSIBLE DESIGN (2010), http://www.ada.gov/2010ADAstandards_index.htm.

32. *See* Indep. Living Res. v. Or. Arena Corp., 1 F. Supp. 2d 1124 (D. Or. 1998).

typically is not considered a dwelling).[33] Single-family residential units are covered by the FHA if they are in buildings of four or more units (e.g., condominiums).[34] In general, the design and construction regulations do not apply to single-family residences, even though anti-discrimination provisions do.[35] Single-family residences funded with public resources or operated by governmental entities may be covered under other elements of federal disability law.

- *The Americans with Disabilities Act of 1990 (ADA).*[36] The ADA prohibits discrimination against people with disabilities in employment, state and local government services, public accommodation, and telecommunications.[37] The ADA was enacted in 1990 and signed into law by President George H.W. Bush.[38] In 2008, President George W. Bush signed the ADA Amendments Act (ADAAA).[39] The ADA requires accessibility. Accessibility guidelines are published by the United States Access Board (USAB) as the ADA Accessibility Guidelines (ADAAG).[40] The ADAAG have been revised and updated since their original development and are now consistent with guidelines

---

33. 42 U.S.C. § 3602 (defining dwelling).

34. 24 C.F.R. § 100.205(d) ex. 1 (2008).

35. SUSSER, *supra* note 13, at § II(F).

36. Americans with Disabilities Act of 1990, Pub. L. No. 101-336, 104 Stat. 327 (codified as amended at 42 U.S.C. § 12101-12213 (2006)). *See generally* BNA, *supra* note 13, *and* SUSSER, *supra* note 13.

37. 42 U.S.C. § 12101.

38. 136 Cong. Rec. S16,826-04 (daily ed. Oct. 23, 1990) (Presidential Approvals).

39. ADA Amendments Act of 2008, Pub. L. No. 110-325, 122 Stat. 3554 (codified as amended at 42 U.S.C. § 12101 et seq. (2006)).

40. UNITED STATES ACCESS BOARD, ADA ACCESSIBILITY GUIDELINES (2002), http://www .access-board.gov/guidelines-and-standards/buildings-and-sites/about-the-ada-standards /background/adaag#2.

for federal facilities that are covered by the ABA.[41] The ADAAG also have been made consistent with the model requirements of the International Building Code.[42] The DOJ also has a detailed publication that addresses the 2010 ADA Standards for Accessible Design.[43]

i. *Title I of the ADA.*[44] Under Title I, employers must provide "reasonable" accommodations to qualified employees with a disability.[45] The reasonable accommodations do not require the employer to take overly costly actions, but they do require the employer to take reasonable steps, which may be something difficult to precisely calculate.[46] Such steps include adjusting the physical work environment of a building or property.[47] The test is one of undue hardship that requires a showing of significant difficulty or expense for compliance.[48] This standard is not easy to meet.

If a building or facility where an accommodation is requested was constructed, altered, renovated, or otherwise built while covered by ADA design guidelines, the ADA design guidelines are required to have been followed in the process.[49] If the guidelines

---

41. *Id.; see also* 42 U.S.C. §§ 4151-4157.

42. International Building Code (2012).

43. U.S. Dep't of Justice, 2010 ADA Standards for Accessible Design (2010), *supra* note 31.

44. Americans with Disabilities Act of 1990, 327 (codified as amended at 42 U.S.C. § 12111-12117 (2006)).

45. *Id.*

46. *Id.*

47. 42 U.S.C. § 12111(9).

48. *Id.* § 12111(10).

49. *Id.* § 12183.

were not followed and a request for an adjustment to accommodate the needs of an employee is made later, the adjustment will not fall within the scope of a reasonable accommodation because it was required initially. This means that the cost limitation of reasonable accommodation would not be applicable to such a change to the building or property. The employer would simply be responsible for not having complied with the requirements of federal disability law.

ii.   *Title II of the ADA.*[50] Title II prohibits discrimination based on disability in programs, services, and activities provided or made available by public entities.[51] Title II is designed to ensure that qualified individuals with disabilities have access to programs, services, and activities of state and local government on a basis that is equal to that of people without disabilities.[52] Part A of Title II covers a general range of programs, services, and activities. Part B of Title II focuses on public transportation.[53] HUD enforces Title II as it relates to state and local public housing, housing assistance, and housing referrals.[54] Title II sets standards of accessibility for public facilities and programs but not for private single-family residential housing.

---

50. Americans with Disabilities Act of 1990, 337-53 (codified as amended at 42 U.S.C. §§ 12131-12161 (2006)).

51. *Id.*

52. 42 U.S.C. § 12101.

53. *Id.* §§ 12131-12134; 12141-12165.

54. *Id.* §§ 12131-12161.

iii. *Title III of the ADA.*[55] Title III prohibits discrimination based on disability in the provision of goods, services, facilities, privileges, advantages, or accommodations of any place of public accommodation by any person owning, leasing, or operating a place of public accommodation.[56] Title III defines public accommodation and provides a list of examples. Private entities and property owners are considered to be operating places of public accommodation when they are open to the public.[57] Places of public accommodation are not government owned or operated as publicly operated facilities and services are covered under Title II. A partial list of examples of places of public accommodation, for illustrative purposes, includes hotels, restaurants, auditoriums, shopping malls, concert halls, retail centers, and banks.[58] Various commercial facilities are also covered under Title III. Commercial facilities are slightly different from places of public accommodation. Although commercial facilities must comply with the new construction and alteration requirements, they do not come within the barrier removal requirements.[59] A commercial facility might be a factory or an office building where the employees are the only people allowed in the facility, but if the facility offers tours to the public or to the

---

55. Americans with Disabilities Act of 1990, 353-365 (codified as amended at 42 U.S.C. §§ 12181-12189 (2006)).

56. *Id.*

57. 42 U.S.C. § 12181(7) (defining public accommodations).

58. *Id.* § 12181(7)(a)-(b), (d)-(e).

59. *Id.* §§ 12182-12183.

extent that it has areas that are open to accommodate a range of people, it is subject to the full requirements of a place of public accommodation.[60] Private clubs are not covered by Title III, unless the club makes its facilities available to nonmembers.[61] A single-family residential house is not considered a place of public accommodation, but if there is a business operating out of part of the house, that part of the building is covered by Title III.[62] A mixed-use hotel development project with an area devoted to residential housing and an area with rooms let out as hotel rooms is subject to Title III with respect to the hotel rooms but subject to the FHA with respect to the residences.[63] A day care center or senior facility run by a church is covered by Title III, but the actual church itself has a religious exemption.[64] Title III requires facilities to be accessible in accordance with ADA guidelines. This means that buildings and facilities need things like ramps, lifts, accessible bathrooms, automatic doors, and readily accessible entranceways. For facilities and structures that predate 1992, barriers to accessibility need to be removed to the extent that doing so is *readily achievable*. When older buildings are altered, at that time, they must be accessible to the *maximum extent possible*.

---

60. 28 C.F.R. § 36 app. C (1991).

61. *Id.* § 36.102(e).

62. *Id.* § 36.207; BNA, *supra* note 13, Introduction to Title III, Adam 30:3.

63. 28 C.F.R. § 36 app. C; BNA, *supra* note 13.

64. 28 C.F.R. § 36 app. C; BNA, *supra* note 13.

iv.   *Title IV of the ADA.*[65] Title IV covers equal access
to telecommunications systems.[66] It may have implications for interconnectivity with respect to com-
munications among various property locations, but
it does not focus on the physical mobility of people
with disabilities.

• *Executive Order 13217.*[67] Executive Order 13217 requires
federal agencies to evaluate their policies and programs
to determine whether any can be revised or modified
to improve the availability of community-based living
arrangements for persons with disabilities.[68] Community-
based living might include senior housing, group homes,
provisions of clinical or health services, and other types of
arrangements that facilitate integrating people with disabilities into the broader community rather than isolating
them in institutions.

As these regulations indicate, the reach of federal disability
law is great. At the same time, the federal regulations touch
only slightly on single-family residential uses. Even when dealing with multi-family housing that is covered by more extensive
inclusive design regulations than single-family housing, there
are limits on the extent that units have to meet universal design
requirements. For example, under HUD regulations, only 5% of

---

65. Americans with Disabilities Act of 1990 at 365 (codified as amended at 42 U.S.C.
§§ 12181-12189 (2006)).

66. *Id.*

67. Exec. Order No. 13217, 3 C.F.R. 774 (2002), *reprinted in* 42 U.S.C. § 12131 (2006).

68. *Id.*; *see* U.S. Dep't of Hous. & Urban Dev., Delivering on the Promise: U.S. Department
of Housing and Urban Development Self Evaluation to Promote Community for People Living with Disabilities, Report to the President on Executive Order 13217 (2002), http://www
.hud.gov/offices/fheo/images/DPromise.pdf.

qualifying public housing units must be fully accessible in terms of "universal design."[69]

The low level of inclusive design in residential housing ignores network effect by failing to address the inability of mobility impaired people to safely and easily socialize and participate at locations that are important to community life. Even if a mobility impaired person's own housing unit is accessible, the housing units of family, friends, and colleagues may not be, and getting from one's own residence to other locations may be difficult. By dramatically limiting single-family residential uses from reasonable inclusive design requirements, such as meeting a visitability standard of accessibility, a significant part of a community's land uses may continue to have barriers to inclusion. Thus, we need to think in broader terms concerning the need for inclusive design housing. We must recognize the public interest in making both publicly and privately funded units, along with multifamily and single-family units, safely and easily navigated by people with low and declining functional mobility.

---

69. There is a standard of 5% or a minimum of at least one dwelling unit that must meet mobility impairment regulations for all projects that receive federal financial assistance, including: Section 202/811 capital advances, Section 8 project-based assistance, newly constructed public housing projects, and public housing projects undergoing rehabilitation that's financed by Comprehensive Improvement Assistance Program (CIAP) funds. *See* U.S. Dep't of Hous. & Urban Dev., Mark-to-Market Program Operating Procedures Guide, app. 1 (attachment B) (DOC 19479.PDF0) (2004), https://www.hud.gov/sites/documents/DOC_19479.PDF and the link to the entire Mark-to-Market procedures is https://www.hud.gov/program_offices/housing/mfh/presrv/presmfh/opglinks The appendix also references, for further definitions, "New Construction (24 C.F.R. § 8.23(b))," "Substantial Alteration (24 C.F.R. § 8.23(a))," and "Other Alterations/Clarifications (24 C.F.R. § 8.23(b))" *Id.* at B-2. Guidelines for meeting mobility impaired regulations are also outlined and are similar to what one might expect from a form of universal design. *Id.* at B-3. *See generally* U.S. Dep't Of Hous. & Urban Dev., Accessibility Requirements For Buildings, https://www.hud.gov/program_offices/fair_housing_equal_opp/disabilities/accessibilityR (last visited Feb. 4, 2020).

A common thread running through each of the identified categories of regulations is the extent to which inclusive design requirements are predicated on the public character of the property in question. The greater the perceived "publicness" of a place, the more extensive the design requirements. This distinction between public and private spaces and places seems to be in large part based on similar distinctions made in other areas of civil rights law. The federal government may prevent people from discriminating against people with disabilities in terms of access to the local courthouse or coffee shop, but it does not prohibit individuals from discriminating against them with respect to who they invite into their private homes. This is the way that race is treated. A place of business cannot refuse service to customers based on race, but individuals are free to not invite people to their homes based on race. To a certain extent, this distinction is because of a concern of protecting an individual's rights of privacy and association.[70]

With respect to residential structures, the concern should be one of making the home safe and easy to navigate for anyone invited onto the property. Accessible design does not require people to invite other people into their homes if they do not want to; rather, it seeks only to make the structure accessible so that, over the life of the structure, it will be usable by many different types of people who may be invited in. Thus, the privacy and associational rights of property owners are not put in

---

70. *See generally* Jennifer Jolly-Ryan, *Chipping Away at Discrimination at the Country Club*, 25 PEPP. L. REV. 495 (1997); Cynthia A. Leiferman, *Private Clubs: A Sanctuary for Discrimination?* 40 BAYLOR L. REV. 71 (1988); Thomas W. Merrill, *Property and the Right to Exclude*, 77 NEB. L. REV. 730 (1998); *and* Lior Jacob Strahilevitz, *Information Asymmetries and the Rights to Exclude*, 104 MICH. L. REV. 1835 (2006).

jeopardy by simply requiring design features that support public health, safety, welfare, and morals.

When dealing with the built environment, all structures and uses have some impact on the overall environment. Making the built environment more accessible and navigable does not violate anyone's right of privacy or association; it simply requires that buildings and uses be developed and coordinated in ways that make a community safe and easy for everyone to navigate. It also means making services, programs, and activities readily available and accessible, with particular attention given to the inclusion of people with disabilities and people aging in place.

The primary focus of this book is the public regulation of land use and thus Title II of the ADA, the FHA, and the RHA. Discussion of Title III of the ADA is limited because Title III covers privately owned places of public accommodation.

4

People Protected Under the ADA, RHA, and FHA

As a land use and zoning professional, it is important to know that there has been a great deal of litigation regarding the determination of who is protected under the various laws that address the rights of people with disabilities. Most of these cases have involved the question of whether an individual qualifies as a person with a disability under these laws. In most land use and zoning cases, zoning officials typically are not presented with complex cases of determining whether a person qualifies as a person with a disability. Instead, they must determine whether and to what extent the disability laws apply to the matter under consideration. Therefore, the details of this litigation are not central to understanding the core issues in the relationship between land use law and disability. The issues typically confronted involve the application of these disability laws to land use planning and zoning when a person is accepted as having a disability. Nonetheless, a professional who works with land use and zoning must acquire a basic understanding of the requirements that need to be considered regarding a person protected by the Americans with Disabilities Act (ADA), the Rehabilitation Act (RHA), or the Fair Housing Act (FHA). It is up to claimants to show that they are entitled to the protection of the disability laws at issue. The ADA, RHA, and FHA each offer a definition of who is intended to be covered by their respective provisions. The Acts are closely similar, and courts tend to treat them alike. Next, this book discusses each of these Acts.

ADA

The ADA protects people with disabilities from discrimination. This means that the meaning of *disability* must be established, and the person in question must meet the requirements for having such a disability. An individual receives no protection from the ADA if the individual's disability falls outside the statutory definition of a disability. The broad definition of *disability* employed by the ADA is applicable to all Titles of the ADA.[71]

> The term "disability" means, with respect to an individual –
>
> (A) a physical or mental impairment that substantially limits one or more major life activities of such individual;
>
> (B) a record of such an impairment; or
>
> (C) being regarded as having such an impairment.[72]

---

71. Widomski v. State Univ. of N.Y. at Orange, 933 F. Supp. 2d 534, 541 (S.D.N.Y. 2013) (citing Toyota Motor Mfg., Ky., Inc. v. Williams, 534 U.S. 184, 201 (2009)); 42 U.S.C. § 12102(4)(A) (2009).

72. 42 U.S.C. § 12102(1).

Thus, there are three categories of classifications of being a person with a disability under the ADA: people are considered "actually impaired" under section (A), having a "record of" impairment under section (B), and "regarded-as" impaired under section (C).[73]

Actually Impaired

For a person to be considered "actually impaired," it must be demonstrated that the person actually has an impairment. Second, it must be demonstrated that the impairment affects at least one major life activity. Third, it is necessary to demonstrate that the impairment substantially limits the named major life activity. The ADA identifies a list of major life activities that is not exhaustive: "caring for oneself, performing manual tasks, seeing, hearing, eating, sleeping, walking, standing, lifting, bending, speaking, breathing, learning, reading, concentrating, thinking, communicating, and working."[74] These activities are considered to be essential to daily life.

The implementation of the ADA Amendments Act (ADAAA), which became effective January 1, 2009, attempted to define the meaning of "substantial limitation." The ADAAA clarified that "an impairment that substantially limits one major life activity need not limit other major life activities in order to be considered a disability."[75] Additionally, "an impairment that is episodic or in remission is a disability if it would substantially limit a major life activity when active."[76]

---

73. *Id.*; MARK C. WEBER, UNDERSTANDING DISABILITY LAW 14 (2007).

74. 42 U.S.C. § 12102(2)(A).

75. *Id.* § 12102(4)(C).

76. *Id.* § 12102(4)(D).

The most significant change in "substantial impairment" litigation occurred by determining that ameliorative effects of mitigating measures can no longer be considered when determining whether an impairment substantially limits a major life activity.[77] Ameliorative action includes medication, equipment, prosthetics (limbs, hearing aids, oxygen, cochlear implants); the use of assistive technology; reasonable accommodations or auxiliary aids or services; or learned or adaptive behavior or modifications.[78] As such, the effective use of an assistive device will not defeat a person's qualification as a person with a disability under the ADA. There is, however, one exception to not taking ameliorative effects of mitigating measures into account: the ameliorative effects of eyeglasses or contact lenses should be considered in determining whether an individual has an impairment that substantially limits a major life activity.[79]

A Record of Impairment

To make a showing that an individual has a "record of" impairment, the individual is required to demonstrate that she has a record or history of impairment, and that the impairment substantially limits a major life activity.[80]

Regarded as Having an Impairment

An individual is "regarded as" having an impairment, for purposes of 42 U.S.C. § 12102(1)(C), when "the individual establishes that he or she has been subjected to an action prohibited

---

77. *Id*. § 12102(4)(E).

78. *Id*. § 12102(4)(E)(i).

79. *Id*. § 12102(4)(E)(ii)-(iii).

80. U.S. Dep't of Justice, The Americans with Disabilities Act - Title II Technical Assistance Manual, ADA.gov, https://www.ada.gov/taman2.html.

under this chapter because of an actual or perceived physical or mental impairment whether or not the impairment limits or is perceived to limit a major life activity."[81] Thus, someone who is perceived by others as being a person with a disability, but who in fact does not have a disability, is still protected from discrimination under the ADA.

To be protected under the ADA, an individual must qualify under the applicable Title of the ADA.

Title II of the ADA applies to government programs, services, and activities provided by public entities. Under Title II, a "qualified individual with a disability means an individual with a disability who, with or without reasonable modifications to rules, policies, or practices, the removal of architectural, communication, or transportation barriers, or the provision of auxiliary aids and services, meets the essential eligibility requirements for the receipt of services or the participation in programs or activities provided by a public entity."[82]

The following conditions are not considered an impairment: homosexuality, bisexuality, transvestism, gender identity disorders, sexual behavior disorders, compulsive gambling, kleptomania, pyromania, and psychoactive substance abuse disorders.[83]

Alcoholism is a condition protected under the ADA.[84]

The ADA, RHA, and FHA deny protection to individuals who currently are engaged in the illegal use of drugs.[85] The "illegal use of drugs" includes the use of any drugs that are considered

---

81. 42 U.S.C. § 12102(3)(A).

82. 29 C.F.R. § 35.104 (2016).

83. 42 U.S.C. § 12211 (2009); 29 U.S.C. § 705(20)(E)-(F) (2014) (applying to Section 504 of the Rehabilitation Act).

84. Mararri v. WCI Steel, 130 F.3d 1180, 1180 (6th Cir. 1997).

85. 42 U.S.C. § 12210(a) (2009); 29 U.S.C. § 705(20)(C)(i).

unlawful under the Controlled Substances Act.[86] However, the ADA and RHA protect individuals who have successfully completed a supervised drug rehabilitation program and who are no longer engaged in the use of illegal drugs, and individuals who are "erroneously regarded" as using illegal drugs.[87]

SECTION 504 OF THE RHA

Similar to the ADA, the RHA protects only individuals who have a qualifying disability.

The RHA defines a disability as:

(A) except as otherwise provided in subparagraph (B), a physical or mental impairment that constitutes or results in a substantial impediment to employment; or

(B) for purposes of sections 701, 711, and 712 of this title and subchapters II, IV, V, and VII, the meaning given it in section 12102 of Title 42 [the ADA].[88]

Therefore, for our purposes concerning the intersection of disability law with land use and zoning, the RHA and the ADA employ the same definition of *disability*.

FHA

The FHA prohibits housing discrimination on the basis of race, color, religion, sex, disability, familial status, or national origin in public and private real estate transactions. The FHA uses the term "handicap" rather than "disability." (The addition of

---

86. 42 U.S.C. § 12210(d)(1); 29 U.S.C. § 705(10).

87. 42 U.S.C. § 12210(b); 29 U.S.C. § 705(20)(C)(ii).

88. 29 U.S.C. § 705(9). An individual with a disability is defined in 29 U.S.C. § 705(20).

language to the FHA to protect people with a handicap was added by the Fair Housing Amendments Act [FHAA].)

The FHA defines a qualified person with a "handicap" as one who has:

(1) a physical or mental impairment which substantially limits one or more of such a person's major life activities,

(2) a record of having such an impairment, or

(3) being regarded as having such an impairment.[89]

The FHA defines *handicap* the same way the ADA and RHA define *disability*. Therefore, case law on the issue of disability under the ADA and RHA will impact cases that arise under the FHA. Under all three Acts, the definition of a person with a disability is virtually the same. Once it is determined that a person is or may be entitled to protection under our disability laws, we must then determine how this will impact land planning, design, and regulation.

---

89. 42 U.S.C. § 3602(h).

5

Coverage of the ADA, RHA, and FHA

Once it is established that a person is protected by the Americans with Disabilities Act (ADA), the Fair Housing Act (FHA), or the Rehabilitation Act (RHA), it is necessary to determine the scope of coverage for each Act in terms of the functions of planning, design, and land regulation. In this chapter, the coverage of each Act is outlined. One should also refer to the description of each of these Acts in chapter 3 and to chapter 4 for additional information about coverage for each Act.

ADA

As to local planning and zoning activities, Title II of the ADA covers "*services, programs* and *activities* provided or made available by public entities."[90] A public entity is defined as

90. 42 U.S.C. § 12132; 38 C.F.R. § 35.102(a).

"(A) any State or local government; (B) any department, agency, special purpose district, or other instrumentality of a State or States or local government; and (C) the National Railroad Passenger Corporation, and any commuter authority (as defined by section 24102(4) of Title 49)."[91]

By this definition, Title II is meant to apply to all state and local governments but not to the federal government. Courts have held that municipal planning and zoning are covered programs, services, or activities under Title II of the ADA.[92] This means that local planning and zoning activities must comply with the ADA.

As to private land regulation, Title III of the ADA covers the provision of *goods, services, facilities, privileges, advantages,* or *accommodations* of *any place of public accommodation.* This applies to private places of public accommodation and to private clubs that open themselves to public events; to residential homes that include a home office or business where members of the public are invited; and to common areas of housing facilities. Title III also has implications for mixed-use hotels, residential housing projects, and for things such as day care and senior facilities. As we plan, design, and regulate for various land uses, we must consider the safe and secure connection among public and private land uses.

RHA

The RHA precludes discrimination against people with disabilities only in "*programs* or *activities*" that receive "federal financial assistance" from a federal agency.[93]

---

91. 42 U.S.C. § 12131.

92. Wis. Cmty. Servs., Inc. v. Milwaukee, 465 F.3d 737, 750 (7th Cir. 2006).

93. 29 U.S.C. § 794(a).

According to the Department of Justice (DOJ) and the Department of Health and Human Services (DHHS) regulations for Section 504 of the RHA, an agency is any federal department that has power "to extend financial assistance."[94] A recipient can be any private or public agency that receives federal financial assistance.[95]

Federal financial assistance is defined as:

> any grant, loan, contract (other than a procurement contract or a contract of insurance or guaranty), or any other arrangement by which the Department provides or otherwise makes available assistance in the form of: (1) funds; (2) services of Federal personnel; or (3) real and personal property or any interest in or use of such property, including: (i) transfers or leases of such property for less than fair market value or for reduced consideration; (ii) and proceeds from a subsequent transfer or lease of such property if the Federal share of its fair market value is not returned to the Federal Government.[96]

Program or activity means that "all of the operations of" the agency receiving financial assistance are required to comply with Section 504 of the RHA, even if part of the agency did not directly receive federal funds.[97] In practice, this also means that if a private corporation receives any federal assistance, or if it provides a public service, the entire corporation is covered by

---

94. 28 C.F.R. § 41.3(c).
95. 28 C.F.R. § 41.3(d); 45 C.F.R. § 84.3(f).
96. 28 C.F.R. § 41.3(e); 45 C.F.R. § 84.3(h).
97. 29 U.S.C. § 794(b).

Section 504. However, if federal assistance is provided only to a "geographically separate facility," only that facility is covered under Section 504.

FHA

Many people familiar with property, housing, and real estate law may already be familiar with the FHA. The FHA covers private housing; housing that receives federal financial assistance; state and local government housing; lending, planning, and zoning practices; new construction design; advertising; and private land regulations, such as those contained in covenants and restrictions or in a declaration of condominium. Basically, the FHA applies to planning, design, and land regulations that hinder a person with a disability from being able to obtain an equal opportunity to acquire and enjoy housing.

6

Anti-Discrimination Provisions

The vast majority of planning, land use, and zoning issues covered under the Americans with Disabilities Act (ADA), the Fair Housing Act (FHA), and the Rehabilitation Act (RHA) relate either to a failure to follow a particular guideline or requirement, or to a claim of discrimination. Failure to follow particular guidelines and requirements of disability law is a matter of non-compliance with the rules.

What often is much more complicated and nuanced than compliance with the regulations is dealing with a claim of discrimination. Discrimination claims often involve the need to evaluate multiple factors. The evidence of discrimination may be less than clear. In dealing with claims of discrimination, the courts use three approaches to evaluate a claim: (1) disparate treatment, (2) disparate impact, and (3) failure to provide a reasonable accommodation or modification. In addressing these methods, it becomes clear that courts treat all three methods the same under each of the Acts.

ADA

The ADA provides that:

> . . . no qualified individual with a disability shall, by reason of such disability, be excluded from participation in or be denied the benefits of services, programs, or activities of a public entity, or be subjected to discrimination by any such entity.[98]

> To prevail under Title II(A), covering public programs, services, and activities, plaintiffs must demonstrate that (1) they are 'qualified individuals' with a disability; (2) that the defendants are subject to the ADA; and (3) that plaintiffs were denied the opportunity to participate in or benefit from defendants' services, programs, or activities, or were otherwise discriminated against by defendants, by reason of plaintiffs' disabilities.[99]

RHA

The RHA says this about discrimination:

> No otherwise qualified individual with a disability in the United States, as defined by section 705(2) of this title, shall solely by reason of her or his disability, be excluded from the participation in, be denied the benefits of, or be

---

98. 42 U.S.C. § 12132.
99. Noel v. NYC Taxi and Limousine Com'n, 687 F.3d 63, 68 (2d Cir. 2012) (quoting Henrietta D. v. Bloomberg, 331 F.3d 261, 272 (2d Cir. 2003)).

subjected to discrimination under any program or activity receiving federal financial assistance or under any program or activity conducted by any Executive agency or the United States Postal Service.[100]

FHA

The FHA states:

It shall be unlawful for any person or other entity whose business includes engaging in residential real estate-related transactions to discriminate against any person in making available such a transaction, or in the terms or conditions of such a transaction, because of race, color, religion, sex, handicap, familial status, or national origin.[101]

It shall be unlawful . . . to discriminate in the sale or rental, or to otherwise make unavailable or deny, a dwelling to any buyer or renter because of a handicap of: (A) that buyer or renter, (B) a person residing in or intending to reside in that dwelling after it is sold, rented or made available; or (C) any person associated with that buyer or renter.[102]

---

100. Rehabilitation Act of 1973, Pub. L. No. 93-112, § 504, 87 Stat. 394 (1973) (codified as amended at 29 U.S.C.§ 794(a)).

101. 42 U.S.C. § 3605.

102. 42 U.S.C. § 3604(f)(1).

7

Methods of Demonstrating Discrimination

There are three approaches to proving a claim of discrimination under the Americans with Disabilities Act (ADA), the Rehabilitation Act (RHA), or the Fair Housing Act (FHA): (1) *disparate treatment*, (2) *disparate impact*, and (3) the *denial of* a legitimate request for *a reasonable accommodation or a reasonable modification*. These claims may arise in a number of common land use and zoning situations.

Planning decisions may be challenged for causing discrimination in housing and for denying equal access to programs, services, and activities. In addition to asserting that certain planning, zoning, or land regulations are in themselves discriminatory with respect to people with disabilities, discrimination also may be asserted when an exception to the stated rules and regulations is not granted or when a request to adjust the built environment is not approved. These requests for exceptions, variances, and modifications must be granted if they are reasonable.

If a request for a reasonable accommodation or modification is not granted, a person protected by disability laws may have an action for discrimination. The obligation to provide a reasonable accommodation or modification applies to public planning and zoning under Title II of the ADA and to private housing and land regulations under the FHA. Therefore, it is important to understand the criteria for determining when and whether a request is reasonable.

A starting place for the broader discussion of methods of demonstrating discrimination is the recent U.S. Supreme Court decision of *Texas Department of Housing and Community Affairs v. Inclusive Communities Project, Inc.*[103] In this case, Inclusive Communities sued the Texas Department of Housing on the ground that the Texas Department of Housing's policy of using tax credits in facilitating the building of affordable housing resulted in continued racial segregation by allocating too many tax credits for housing construction in predominantly black inner-city neighborhoods and not enough for construction of affordable housing in suburban areas.[104] The case went to the U.S. Supreme Court on a claim of discrimination under disparate impact rather than under disparate treatment.[105] A disparate treatment claim would require a showing of an intent to discriminate in the process of making affordable housing available to everyone, whereas a disparate impact approach does not require a showing of discriminatory intent.[106]

The issue in *Inclusive Communities* was whether the facially neutral policy of awarding tax credits for construction

---

103. *See* Texas Dep't of Hous. & Cmty. Affairs v. Inclusive Communities Project, Inc., 135 S.Ct. 2507 (2015).
104. *Id.* at 2514.
105. *Id.* at 2514.
106. *Id.* at 2513.

of affordable housing resulted in outcomes that continued to segregate the urban area by race, with blacks overrepresented in the inner city and underrepresented in the suburbs.[107] After examining the history and language of the legislation, the Court found that the FHA addressed discriminatory outcomes *and* intentions.[108] This means that a land use policy that is neutral on its face and that is not passed with animus against a particular class of people is still potentially discriminatory if it produces outcomes that are different for different identifiable groups.

Disparate treatment analysis requires a comparison of groups by using statistical evidence that indicates that the disparate outcome between the groups has a causal connection to a land use or housing policy.[109] The causal connection must be more than casual.[110]

As stated in the *Inclusive Communities* opinion:

> . . . a disparate-impact claim that relies on a statistical disparity must fail if the plaintiff cannot point to a defendant's policy or policies causing that disparity. A robust causality requirement ensures that "[r]acial imbalance . . . does not, without more, establish a prima facie case of disparate impact" and thus protects defendants from being held liable for racial disparities they did not create.[111]

Disparate impact analysis is designed to address zoning laws and housing practices that result in the exclusion of minorities

---

107. *Id*. at 2513.
108. *Id*. at 2511-12.
109. *Id*. at 2522.
110. *Id*. at 2523-24.
111. *Id*. at 2523 (quoting Wards Cove Packing Co. v. Atonio, 490 U.S. 642, 653 (1989)).

from certain neighborhoods without a sufficient constitutional justification. In defending against a disparate impact claim, local officials and developers have leeway to provide explanations for policies and practices. Appropriate explanations and justifications might make the policies and practices acceptable, even if there is a statistical difference in outcome between identifiable comparison groups.

In the context of disability law, we are considering the public and private land policies and practices that have a disparate impact on people with disabilities compared to people not protected by disability law.

In examining the three methods of demonstrating discrimination, the focus must first be on the activities that come within the coverage of each of the primary Acts: the ADA, the RHA, and the FHA. The ADA and RHA prohibit discrimination in the *programs*, *services*, or *activities* of public entities. The FHA covers discrimination in the *selling*, *leasing*, *advertising*, and *financing* of housing.

Innovative Health Systems v. City of White Plains explains "programs, activities, and services and the application of the ADA to local planning and zoning":[112]

Both Title II of the ADA and Section 504 of the RHA prohibit discrimination based on a disability by a public entity.[113]

The ADA does not explicitly define "services, programs, or activities". . . . the Rehabilitation Act, however, defines "program or activity" as "all of the operations" of

---

112. Innovative Health Systems v. City of White Plains, 117 F. 3d 37, 44-45 (2d Cir. 1997).
113. *Id*. at 44.

specific entities, including "a department, agency, special purpose district, or other instrumentality of a State or of a local government."[114] Further, as the district court recognized, the plain meaning of "activity" is a "natural or normal function or operation."[115] Thus, as the district court held, both the ADA and the RHA clearly encompass zoning decisions by the City because making such decisions is a normal function of a governmental entity.[116] Moreover, as the district court also noted, the language of Title II's anti-discrimination provision does not limit the ADA's coverage to conduct that occurs in the "programs, services, or activities" of the City.[117]

As the preamble to the Department of Justice regulations explains, "Title II applies to anything a public entity does. . . . All governmental activities of public entities are covered."[118] The Department of Justice's Technical Assistance Manual, which interprets its regulations, specifically refers to zoning as an example of a public entity's obligation to modify its policies, practices, and procedures to avoid discrimination.[119]

Next, this book addresses additional details related to discriminations by disparate treatment, disparate impact, and failure to provide a reasonable accommodation/modification.

---

114. *Id.* (quoting 29 U.S.C. § 794(b)(1)(A) (1994)).
115. *Id.*
116. *Id.*
117. *Id.* at 44-45.
118. *Id.* at 45.
119. *Id.*

DISPARATE TREATMENT (INTENTIONAL DISCRIMINATION)

Quoting from the opinion in *Candlehouse, Inc. v. Town of Vestal, NY:*[120]

> Claims of intentional discrimination are properly analyzed utilizing the familiar, burden shifting model developed by the courts for use in employment discrimination settings dating back to the Supreme Court's decision in McDonnell Douglas Corp. v. Green, 411 U.S. 792, 93 S.Ct. 1817, 36 L.Ed.2d 668 (1973). Under that analysis, a plaintiff must first establish a prima facie case of intentional discrimination . . . by "present[ing] evidence that animus against the protected group was a significant factor in the position taken by the municipal decision-makers themselves or by those to whom the decision makers were knowingly responsive." Once a plaintiff makes out its prima facie case, "the burden of production shifts to the defendants to provide a legitimate, nondiscriminatory reason for their decision." "The plaintiff must then prove that the defendants intentionally discriminated against them on a prohibited ground." The fact-finder is permitted "to infer the ultimate fact of discrimination"

---

120. 2013 WL 1867114 (N.D.N.Y. May 3, 2013). *See also* Cinnamon Hills Youth Crisis Ctrs., Inc. v. Saint George City, 685 F.3d 917 (10th Cir. 2012); Nikolich v. Village of Arlington Heights, Ill., 870 F. Supp. 2d 556 (N.D. Ill 2012); Rise, Inc. v. Malheur County, 2012 WL 1085501 (D. Or. Feb. 13, 2012); 10th Street Partners, LLC v. County Commission of Sarasota, Florida, 2012 WL 4328655 (M.D. Fla. Sept. 20, 2012); U.S. v. City of Baltimore, 845 F. Supp. 2d 640 (D. Md. 2012); Get Back Up, Inc. v. City of Detroit, 2015 WL 1089662 (6th Cir. Unpub. 2015) (failure to demonstrate discriminatory intent); *and* Get Back Up, Inc. v. City of Detroit, 2018 WL 1568528 (6th Cir. 2018). (Discriminatory opposition to the placement of a drug and alcohol rehabilitation facility by members of the public does not automatically direct a zoning decision. Also, rational justifications that are given denial of the use do not violate the ADA or FHA.) MALLOY, *supra* note 1.

if the plaintiff has made "a substantial showing that the defendants' proffered explanation was false."

The key inquiry in the intentional discrimination analysis is whether discriminatory animus was a motivating factor behind the decision at issue. The Second Circuit has identified the following five factors a fact-finder may consider in evaluating a claim of intentional discrimination:

(1) the discriminatory impact of the governmental decision; (2) the decision's historical background; (3) the specific sequence of events leading up to the challenged decision; (4) departures from the normal procedural sequences; and (5) departures from normal substantive criteria.[121]

DISPARATE IMPACT

The most important case on disparate impact analysis is the *Inclusive Communities* case discussed earlier in this chapter. Other cases also do a good job of explaining disparate impact. One good example is from the case discussed next.

Quoting from the opinion in *Candlehouse*:[122]

To establish a prima facie case under this theory, the plaintiff must show: (1) the occurrence of certain outwardly neutral practices, and (2) a significantly adverse or disproportionate impact on persons of a particular

---

121. *Candlehouse, Inc.*, 2013 WL 1867114.

122. *Id*. Note that at the time of this court decision, the use of disparate impact analysis under the FHA was still contested. The U.S. Supreme Court answered this question by permitting disparate impact analysis under careful limitations. *See Texas Dep't of Hous.*, 135 S.Ct. at 2511-12.

type produced by the defendant's facially neutral acts or practices. . . . A plaintiff need not show the defendant's action was based on any discriminatory intent. . . . To prove that a neutral practice has a significantly adverse or disproportionate impact. . . . on a protected group, a plaintiff must prove the practice actually or predictably results in discrimination. . . . In addition, a plaintiff must prove "a causal connection between the facially neutral policy and the alleged discriminatory effect." Once a plaintiff establishes its prima facie case, "the burden shifts to the defendant to prove that its actions furthered, in theory and in practice, a legitimate, bona fide governmental interest and that no alternative would serve that interest with less discriminatory effect."

The basis for a successful disparate impact claim involves a comparison between two groups—those affected and those unaffected by the facially neutral policy. This comparison must reveal that although neutral, the policy in question imposes a significantly adverse or disproportionate impact on a protected group of individuals.

Statistical evidence is . . . normally used in cases involving fair housing disparate impact claims. Although there may be cases where statistics are not necessary, there must be some analytical mechanism to determine disproportionate impact.

FAILURE TO PROVIDE A REASONABLE ACCOMMODATION OR REASONABLE MODIFICATION

The third method of demonstrating discrimination is by showing that a person has been denied a request for a reasonable accommodation or modification. The requirements for a reasonable accommodation or modification are set out in each of the ADA, the FHA, and the RHA. In general, the difference between accommodation and modification is that accommodations are made in terms of adjusting things, such as rules, regulations, covenants, and restrictions, whereas modifications are made to physical environments, such as buildings, offices, rooms, work equipment, and parking spaces. A request for a reasonable accommodation or modification is essentially a request for an exception to the rules. In this regard, a request for reasonable accommodation or modification sometimes is confused with being a zoning variance when a request for an exception is made to a zoning board or to a homeowners association (HOA) board. However, a request for a reasonable accommodation is not a zoning variance in the typical sense of land use and zoning law, and it needs to be treated differently in terms of the relevant legal rules that apply.

If a zoning board of appeal is presented with a request for a variance (an area variance or a use variance), the local zoning code and state law related to variances applies. If the issue involves private land regulations and the request is made to a HOA board, the granting of an exception will be governed by the criteria set out in the restrictive regulations that govern the property. As to zoning, an area variance typically involves a request for an exception to the regulations addressing things such as the height and size of a structure, setbacks of structures from the property lines, the placement of fences, and approval of accessory structures. Use variances typically involve a request to allow a use in a zone or area where the use is otherwise prohibited by land regulations. In each case, state and local law provide particular criteria to use in consideration of a request for either an area or a use variance. Traditionally, a request for an area variance must be based on demonstrating *practical difficulties* in complying with the land regulation in question.[123] The practical difficulties must not be self-created. As to a use variance, the traditional approach requires the property owner to demonstrate that compliance with the regulations imposes an *unnecessary hardship*. Like the case for an area variance, the unnecessary hardship cannot be self-created.[124] If a variance request is approved or denied, it must be done on findings directly related to the criteria set out to be considered in the variance law. If a denial is appealed, the determination generally will be subject to review to evaluate whether the denial is

---

123. New York law establishes five factors to guide decision makers on area variances. In considering the following criteria, a zoning board is to grant an area variance if, on balance, the benefits to the property owner outweigh the detriments to the neighborhood or community:

1) Whether an undesirable change will be produced in the character of the neighborhood or a detriment to nearby properties will be created by granting the area variance
2) Whether the benefits sought by the applicant can be achieved by some method feasible for the applicant to pursue, other than the area variance
3) Whether the requested variance is substantial
4) Whether the proposed variance will have an adverse effect or impact on the physical or environmental conditions in the neighborhood or district
5) Whether the alleged difficulty was self-created, which consideration shall be relevant to the decision of the board of appeals but shall not necessarily preclude the granting of the area variance

N.Y. Town Law § 267-b (3) (McKinney 2006); Patricia E. Salkin, New York Zoning Law and Practice § 29:12 (4th ed. 2009).

124. In the State of New York, the traditional test of unnecessary hardship has been clarified by statute and requires that the applicant demonstrate all four of the following factors. It is not a balancing test.

1) The applicant cannot realize a reasonable return [for every permitted use of the property], provided that lack of return is substantial as demonstrated by competent financial evidence.
2) The alleged hardship relating to the property in question is unique and does not apply to a substantial portion of the district or neighborhood.
3) The required use variance, if granted, will not alter the essential character of the neighborhood.
4) The alleged hardship has not been self-created.

N.Y. Town Law § 267-b (2) (McKinney 2006).

rationally based on a proper application of the law and supported by competent evidence on the record. A variance request as to private land regulations will be evaluated with reference to the identified private criteria and generally will be reviewed for reasonableness with reference to the business judgment rule.

In the zoning context, and with land regulation more generally, if the request for a variance is granted, the variance is traditionally held to "run with the land," meaning that the variance continues with the property, even if the property is transferred to a new owner at a later date. In other words, the variance is linked to the property and is not personal to the original petitioner that is granted the variance. This elevates the importance of a variance because it will affect the property for a long period of time.

In contrast with a variance, the request for a reasonable accommodation or modification is a request for an exception based on the criteria established under our disability laws, rather than under the state and local law applicable to a planning or zoning variance or under the criteria for a variance set out in private land regulations. When a reasonable accommodation or modification is requested, it is essentially a request for an interpretation of the code and the rules in light of disability laws. The exception should be understood as an interpretation of a reasonable accommodation or modification in light of the land regulation in question and with reference to the disability of the specific person and situation being evaluated. If the request is approved, it should be considered personal to the individual and therefore should not run with the land; it would not be granting a variance but an interpretation of the land regulation in light of the specific facts of the case and the meaning of a reasonable accommodation or modification under these circumstances. If the request for a reasonable accommodation/modification is denied, it will be subject to review under disability law. In this case, the review will be focused on the specific criteria applicable to a request for a reasonable accommodation or modification. The failure to provide a reasonable accommodation or modification will result in evidence not only of a failure to grant an appropriate exception in the land regulation, but in a claim for discrimination in violation of disability laws.

Discrimination against a protected person in a 'suspect' class is typically subject to strict scrutiny review under constitutional law. The Supreme Court, however, has never held that disability is a suspect classification. In disability cases, the courts use a lower standard. They use the standard of a rational basis supported by substantial competent evidence on the record. Some people question the application of this lower standard, and believe that a person with a disability ought to have a decision reviewed under a higher level of scrutiny than that applicable to a variance. Even though this is not the case, the actual standard of review seems higher than for a variance because the decision has to go through the three-factor criteria in evaluating a requested accommodation/modification, and this is in itself a higher standard of evaluation than that of the typical zoning variance request.

On a practical planning level, many people may view requests for variances and exceptions for a reasonable accommodation or modification as disruptive to the planning and zoning process. Planning and zoning are, after all, based on the idea that planning adds stability and predictability to community life by coordinating and meeting a variety of private and public rights with respect to land uses and property development. Land use and zoning is supposed to consider decisions about property use without being driven by who owns the property. In other words, land use planning and zoning is about coordinating land uses in a way that best serves the public health, safety, welfare, and morals, without regard to the particular identity of the property owners. Granting a request for a reasonable accommodation or modification involves making an exception to the planning and zoning rules based on the personal characteristics and situation of an identified person or group of people. Even though the accommodation or modification is made to advance inclusion and to protect the rights of people with disabilities, it may still be the potential source for rethinking the viability and wisdom of an earlier planning and zoning decision. While this is often for the better, it may still be perceived as disruptive and as a source of planning instability. Property, land use, and zoning professionals have to account for the disability laws when planning and making decisions, and should also look at these situations as opportunities for improvement that will enhance community life more generally.

As a preliminary matter to making a case of discrimination based on the denial of a reasonable accommodation/modification, the petitioner must demonstrate that she has standing, she is a person protected by the disability law cited, and she made a request for an accommodation or modification that was denied. It is important to note that, in addition to the standard standing to sue issues, the petitioner must present evidence that she is a person with a disability protected by the ADA, FHA, or RHA. In addition, a petitioner must affirmatively make a request for the accommodation or modification.

There is general agreement in judicial opinions that granting a request for a reasonable accommodation must meet three criteria. Disagreement arises with respect to how these criteria are defined and applied in a given case. The three criteria are: (1) it must be reasonable (as demonstrated by a cost and benefit analysis); (2) it must be necessary (applying a "but for" test); and

(3) it must not fundamentally alter the program, service, activity, or plan from which the exception is being requested.

Quoting from *Austin v. Town of Farmington*:[125]

Reasonableness analysis is "highly fact-specific, requiring a case-by-case determination". . . . A requested accommodation is reasonable where the cost is modest and it does not pose an undue hardship or substantial burden on the rule maker. . . . [An] accommodation is not reasonable "if it would impose an undue financial and administrative burden on the [rule maker] or it would fundamentally alter the nature of the [rule maker's] operations"). Applied to the context of land-use regulations, relevant factors may include the purposes of the restriction, the strength of the Town's interest in the land-use regulation at issue, the need for uniformity, the effect of allowing later landowners without a disability to enjoy the lack of the [same restriction], while all their neighbors are subject to it, the likelihood that a permanent variance will cause other landowners subject to the regulation to seek similar variances, etc.

Here, we explore the criteria for granting, and in the alternative, denying, a reasonable accommodation or modification.

To begin to clarify the requirements for making out a claim for a reasonable accommodation or modification, let us examine a few exemplary court opinions. First, quoting from the

---

125. Austin v. Town of Farmington, 826 F.3d 622 (2d Cir. 2016).

opinion in *Cinnamon Hills Youth Crisis Centers, Inc. v. Saint George City*:[126]

> A claim for reasonable accommodation . . . does not require the plaintiff to prove that the challenged policy intended to discriminate or that in effect it works systematically to exclude the disabled. Instead, in the words of the FHA, a reasonable accommodation is required whenever it "may be necessary to afford [a disabled] person equal opportunity to use and enjoy a dwelling." 42 U.S.C. § 3604(f)(3)(B).
>
> What does it mean to be "necessary"? The word implies more than something merely helpful or conducive. It suggests instead something "indispensable," "essential," something that "cannot be done without." . . . What's more, the FHA's necessity requirement doesn't appear in a statutory vacuum, but is expressly linked to the goal of "afford[ing] . . . equal opportunity to use and enjoy a dwelling." 42 U.S.C. § 3604(f)(3)(B). And this makes clear that the object of the statute's necessity requirement is a level playing field in housing for the disabled. Put simply, the statute requires accommodations that are necessary (or indispensable or essential) to achieving the objective of equal housing opportunities between those with disabilities and those without. *See Bryant Woods Inn, Inc. v. Howard County, Md.*, 124 F.3d 597, 605 (4th Cir.1997); *Schwarz*, 544 F.3d at 1227.

---

126. *Cinnamon Hills*, 685 F.3d at 922-23.

Of course, in some sense all reasonable accommodations treat the disabled not just equally but preferentially. Think of the blind woman who obtains an exemption from a "no pets" policy for her seeing eye dog, or the paraplegic granted special permission to live on a first floor apartment because he cannot climb the stairs. But without an accommodation, those individuals cannot take advantage of the opportunity (available to those without disabilities) to live in those housing facilities. And they cannot because of conditions created by their disabilities. . . . But while the FHA requires accommodations necessary to ensure the disabled receive the same housing opportunities as everybody else, it does not require more or better opportunities. The law requires accommodations overcoming barriers, imposed by the disability, that prevent the disabled from obtaining a housing opportunity others can access. But when there is no comparable housing opportunity for non-disabled people, the failure to create an opportunity for disabled people cannot be called necessary to achieve equality of opportunity in any sense. So, for example, a city need not allow the construction of a group home for the disabled in a commercial area where nobody, disabled or otherwise, is allowed to live.

Requesting a reasonable accommodation for financial feasibility reasons does not qualify as a necessary accommodation.[127] The fact that a person with a disability may prefer to

---

127. *Nikolich,* 870 F. Supp. 2d at 565. In this case, a developer sought an accommodation to permit a 30-unit apartment building for people with mental illness when the zoning code permitted only group homes of up to eight mentally disabled residents. The developer did not show that having more units would better serve the disability needs of the resident but did

conduct a use of property in a less costly way or that a given project would be more economically feasible if done on a larger scale does not make the use necessary for FHA purposes. Thus, the use need not be approved by local zoning officials who are otherwise validly acting in accordance with the police power. At the same time, local zoning officials must show a willingness to take modest steps to accommodate a person with a disability as long as the steps do not pose an undue hardship or a substantial burden on the exercise of their planning and zoning authority.[128]

When a planning board or zoning board of appeal is presented with a claim for a reasonable accommodation, the board must make specific findings. First, the board should assess the application of the various disability laws to the applicant raising the claim—that is, it must conclude that the applicant is a person protected under our disability laws. Second, it should proceed to evaluate the criteria for an accommodation determining: (1) is it reasonable, (2) is it necessary, and (3) does it fundamentally alter the planning and zoning scheme. No single factor seems to trump the evaluation of the request. Findings should be made on each of the criteria, and then, a rational decision should be made based on substantial competent evidence on the record. Reasons and justification for the decision should be included:

A claim for reasonable accommodation . . . does not require the plaintiff to prove that the challenged policy

---

show that the larger building would make the developer's business more efficient and that scaling up would result in lowering the costs per unit. This would make the costs per unit more affordable. The fact that the developer could operate more efficiently or that the units could be lower priced did not satisfy the requirements for the requested accommodation.
128. *Candlehouse*, 2013 WL 1867114, at *15. *See also* 901 Ernston Rd. v. Borough of Sayre Ville Zoning Board of Adjustment, 2018 WL 2176175 (D. NJ 2018).

intended to discriminate or that in effect it works systematically to exclude the disabled. Instead, the FHA provides that a reasonable accommodation is required whenever it may be necessary to afford a person with a disability an equal opportunity to use and enjoy a dwelling.[129]

There is a similar duty to make a reasonable accommodation under both Section 504 of the RHA and the FHA.[130] There is no specific reasonable accommodation requirement in Title II of the ADA, but the U.S. Attorney General has issued implementing regulations that outline the duty of public entities to make reasonable accommodations for people with disabilities. Unlike Title I and Title III of the ADA, Title II does not contain a specific accommodation requirement. The U.S. Attorney General issued implementing regulations at the instruction of Congress. The courts have held that the ADA includes a requirement to provide reasonable accommodations and modifications.[131] The relevant Title II regulations state:

A public entity shall make reasonable modifications in policies, practices, or procedures where the modifications are necessary to avoid discrimination on the basis of disability unless the public entity can demonstrate that making the modifications would fundamentally alter the nature of the service, program or activity.[132]

---

129. *Cinnamon Hills*, 685 F. 3d at 917. MALLOY, *supra* note 1, at 145.

130. *Wis. Cmty. Servs.*, 465 F.3d at 746.

131. *Id.* at 750-51.

132. *Id.* at 751 (quoting 28 Code of Federal Regulations (C.F.R.) § 35.130(b)(7)) [the ADA]. *See also* Palm Partners, LLC v. City of Oakland Park, 102 F. Supp. 3d 1334 (S.D. Fla. 2015) (accommodation not required if it will fundamentally alter the plan).

Regulations require recipients of federal funds to make reasonable accommodation . . . unless the recipient can demonstrate that the accommodation would impose an undue hardship on the operation of the program.[133]

"The Supreme Court has located a duty to accommodate in the statute generally."[134] The ADA and the RHA both impose statutory obligations on public entities to provide reasonable accommodations to persons protected by the Acts. Requesting a reasonable accommodation for financial feasibility reasons does not qualify as a necessary accommodation.[135]

There is some discussion of how the FHA deals with discrimination in housing finance. The FHA in 42 U.S.C. § 3604 requires a reasonable accommodation in sales, rentals, and the offering of housing, but 42 U.S.C. § 3605, a section on financing, does not include the reasonable accommodation language. Because §3605 does not include the language relating to accommodation for mortgage financing, cases have said that there is no obligation to make reasonable accommodations or modifications in the loan qualification requirements or with respect to foreclosure procedures and requirements. This is true even when a plaintiff asserts that she is unable to pay or qualify for a loan due to low income or another cause that directly relates to her disability. Thus, lenders may proceed under their standard mortgage practices in terms of credit qualification requirements and dealing with defaults that go to foreclosure.

---

133. *Id*. at 747 (quoting 28 C.F.R. § 41.53) [the RHA].

134. *Id*.

135. MALLOY, *supra* note 1, at 146.

REASONABLE MODIFICATION

A reasonable modification is treated similarly to a reasonable accommodation. In practice, courts have treated modifications, such as modifying an entranceway by making it wider and by eliminating a step-up at an entranceway, as changes to the physical environment.[136] In contrast, an adjustment in a rule or a practice often is treated as a reasonable accommodation. One does, however, sometimes encounter discussion that reference making a reasonable modification to a rule or a practice rather than limiting that phrasing to physical changes to the environment.

A reasonable modification also applies to Title III of the ADA, which governs privately owned places of public accommodation:

A public accommodation shall make reasonable modifications in policies, practices, or procedures, when the modifications are necessary to afford goods, services, facilities, privileges, advantages, or accommodations to individuals with disabilities, unless the public accommodation can demonstrate that making the modifications would fundamentally alter the nature of the goods, services, facilities, privileges, advantages, or accommodations.[137]

Under the FHA:

Discrimination includes a refusal to permit, at the expense of the handicapped person, reasonable modifications of existing premises occupied or to be occupied by

---

136. Fair Hous. Bd. v. Windsor Plaza Condo., 768 S.E.2d 79, 87 (Va. 2014).
137. 28 C.F.R. 36.302(a).

such person if such modifications may be necessary to afford such person full enjoyment of the premises, except that, in the case of a rental, the landlord may where it is reasonable to do so condition permission for a modification on the renter agreeing to restore the interior of the premises to the condition that existed before the modification, reasonable wear and tear excepted.[138]

A "modification means any change to the public or common use areas of a building or any change to a dwelling unit."[139]

NEED FOR GREATER CLARITY

In spite of the developing case law in this area, in many situations, there is still a lack of certainty as to the evaluation of a claim for a reasonable accommodation or modification. While the three basic criteria for a reasonable accommodation or modification are generally agreed upon, determining exactly how the various criteria should be evaluated and weighed is still unclear. For this reason, it is useful to summarize what is known and to set out some of what remains unresolved.

First, consider the burden of proof. In general, the initial burden of making a prima facie case that a request meets the three criteria for a reasonable accommodation or modification rests with the petitioner.[140] Once a prima facie case is made, the burden shifts back to the respondent to show that the request does not meet the criteria.[141] In contrast to cases that apply the

---

138. 42 U.S.C. § 3604(f)(3)(A).
139. 24 C.F.R. § 100.201.
140. *Lapid-Laurel*, 284 F.3d 442, 458.
141. *Id.*

shifting test to all three criteria, some courts have held that the petitioner has the burden of proving necessity and that as to this criterion, it does not shift to the respondent.[142] Thus, it is not clear how this element will be treated in any given case. The respondent should, nonetheless, respond in order to negate the claim of necessity and also counter the claim by showing that other alternatives are available to address the petitioner's needs.

Looking more closely at each of the three criteria, let us begin with the criteria of reasonableness. In determining whether a request is reasonable, a cost and benefit analysis must be done with respect to the benefit to the petitioner and the costs to the respondent.[143] This should be done in real dollar and cents terms, with evidence of actual and estimated costs and benefits presented for evaluation.[144] The calculation probably does not need to be exact because it is not simply a straightforward calculus, but dollars and cents evidence coupled with a rough sense of justice in a given situation must indicate that the benefits to the petitioner outweigh the costs to the respondent. Another way to consider reasonableness is that the requested accommodation or modification should not impose an *undue financial hardship* or a *substantial administrative burden* on the respondent. Note that this criterion permits reasonable costs and burdens to be imposed on a respondent, so respondent cannot simply argue that making the accommodation or modification will cost him money or impose administrative burdens on his operation.[145] The case must be made that the costs and burdens are unreasonable

---

142. Cimarron Foothills Cmty. Ass'n v. Kippen, 79 P.3d 1214, 1218 (Az. Ct. App. 2003).

143. Vande Zande v. Wisconsin, 44 F.3d 538, 542 (7th Cir. 1995).

144. Reed v. Lepage Bakeries, Inc., 244 F.3d 254, 260 (1st Cir. 2001).

145. Giebeler v. M & B Assocs., 343 F.3d 1143, 1158 (9th Cir. 2003).

in the given situation.[146] Some cases seem to treat undue financial hardship or substantial administrative burden as separate from a cost and benefit analysis. In the Title I employment area, there are cases that indicate that the plaintiff has the burden of making out a plausible and prima facie case that she is making a reasonable request for an accommodation/modification that will assist her. In demonstrating reasonableness, plaintiff must include some basic cost information and suggest that the costs are outweighed by the benefits. The defendant can then respond with additional information and use this information to show that the request is unreasonable. The defendant may also argue, without necessarily demonstrating that the costs outweigh the benefits, that the request imposes an undue financial hardship or a substantial administrative burden. This may be enough for the defendant to win without demonstrating that costs are greater than the benefits. It should be reasonable to borrow from the Title I employment situation when interpreting a similar issue under Title II. Therefore, it seems that evidence of undue financial burden and substantial administrative burden are cost and benefit–oriented assessments.

In considering the calculation of costs and burdens, the question arises as to the relevant reference point of consideration. Are the costs and burdens calculated only with reference to the respondent's business or situation, in terms of the cost structure of the industry (in a commercial setting), or with reference to what other property owners experience more generally in terms of costs and burdens? In other words, should an outcome on this criterion be driven by the fact that a particular respondent

---

146. Goner v. Golden Gate Gardens Apts., 250 F.3d 1039, 1044 (6th Cir. 2001) (citing Hovsons, Inc. v. Twp. of Brick, 89 F.3d 1096, 1104 (3d Cir. 1996)).

has higher costs and perhaps greater inefficiencies than the normal respondent in his position? Should the evaluator consider only the reasonableness in terms of the respondent's costs,[147] or include evaluation of the respondent's costs in relationship to the costs of others? The answer to this seems unclear. Perhaps, the respondent should have to demonstrate that its costs are reasonable relative to the costs and burdens experienced by others who are similarly situated, and that allowance should be given for rough variations within a market sample of providers.

Finally, an issue arises with respect to what it is that has to actually be evaluated for reasonableness. Is a request considered only on its own merits to determine whether it is reasonable, or does it need to be evaluated in light of potential alternatives for addressing the petitioner's needs? For example, let us assume that I live in a condominium that has a rule prohibiting individual unit owners from leaving or storing personal items in the common areas. Nonetheless, I use a walker and want to leave my walker in a corner of the entrance lobby to the condominium building for ease of access when I return from being taken outside the building by caretakers. I request a reasonable accommodation to the rules that will permit me to leave my personal walker in a common area. The determination of reasonableness then raises the question of whether we evaluate only this specific request for reasonableness, or if we evaluate the specific request along with potential alternatives that might indicate that there is a less costly or less intrusive way for me to achieve the same benefit. Stated differently, can the condominium board deny a specific request by offering an alternative that is less costly and less burdensome than the original request, or must it focus only

---

147. *See* U.S. Airways, Inc. v. Barnett, 535 U.S. 391, 405 (2002).

on the question of the reasonableness of the petitioner's specific request? In part, this matter seems to be interconnected with the criterion of necessity.[148]

Sometimes, courts seem to collapse the evaluation of reasonableness and necessity, but it is important to understand them individually and appreciate the relationship between the two concepts. In order for a requested accommodation or modification to be reasonable, it must also be necessary. This necessity test is said to be a "but for" test, as traditionally applied in an FHA situation. This is the case even when the claim is asserted under the ADA and RHA. The claim would be that "but for" granting this request, the petitioner cannot enjoy an equal opportunity for housing or the use and enjoyment of her property. In this claim, there must be evidence of a causal connection between the petitioner's specific disability and the petitioner's requested accommodation or modification. In other words, the accommodation or modification must bear a reasonable nexus to the disability being addressed by the request.

A second element of the necessity test is that it must focus on an *equal opportunity* to *obtain*, *use*, or *enjoy* housing or other property in the same way as other similarly situated people who do not have a disability. It is not about obtaining preferential treatment because of a disability, even though the accommodation or modification may create different treatment—an exception to the rule that is otherwise applicable—because it is done to provide an equal but not preferential opportunity for the petitioner. It is not designed to provide the petitioner with an

---

148. Vorchheimer v. Philadelphian Owners Assoc., 903 F.3d 100 (3d. Cir. 2018). (Petitioner was not allowed to leave his walker in the common area. The denial of the accommodation by the HOA was upheld.)

advantage over others, but instead, to equalize the petitioner's opportunity to use, enjoy, and own property.

As a necessity, the request cannot be simply a preference of the petitioner. This is a key factor that links back to the criterion of reasonableness. In considering the necessity of a request, it seems appropriate to consider alternative ways of accomplishing the same goal. If the same goal might be accomplished in several reasonably satisfactory ways, it is difficult to claim that only one, specific means of accomplishing the goal meets the need. Consequently, if there are multiple ways of meeting the need, no one way is necessary. This means that alternatives should be considered on the question of necessity. When alternatives are on the table, the matter of reasonableness is revisited. The follow-up question is that, if there are several reasonable ways of responding to petitioner's request, why should the respondent have to take on a costlier response when a reasonable and lower-cost response is available? This does not mean that a respondent has a right to demand that he or she be responsible only for the least costly response. It means only that in evaluating the overall reasonableness of a request, a decision maker should consider alternatives and their respective cost as part of making a just and rational response.

Finally, when considering the question of necessity, one must ask whether the harm that the petitioner complains of is one that is common to the general public. For example, assume a petitioner wants to add an entrance ramp to the front entrance of a house to accommodate her need for easy and safe entry to and exit from her home now that she is using a wheelchair. The ramp will be a structure that extends forward from the foundation of the house by 40 feet. Assume further that a front yard setback requires all structures to be at least 30 feet back from the front lot line. With the ramp, the setback will be violated by 10 feet.

In this case, the petitioner might request a reasonable accommodation for an exception to the 30-foot setback so she can modify
her front entrance. Without the ramp, she will not be able to
safely and easily enter and exit her home. Now, assume that the
setback exception will be granted as a reasonable accommodation, but on the condition that certain materials and design features be used, so the ramp blends in with the style and materials
used on the house and in the neighborhood. In this community,
this condition is considered to be a standard condition when a
property owner is approved to add an exterior feature or addition to a home. The petitioner complains that the required design
and materials make the ramp more expensive than it otherwise
might be, and that she should not be required to build an expensive ramp when she can have a friend construct an adequate one
out of unfinished two-by-fours for half the cost. While the petitioner in this case may have a claim for the exception to build the
ramp, the complaint about the cost of an exterior modification
or addition to the home is something experienced by everyone in
the neighborhood. Complying with design and material regulations may not be the lowest cost way to achieve a goal, but it is a
reasonable regulation of property. The higher cost of compliance
related to imposing conditions on design and materials is experienced by everyone in the community, as are the aesthetic benefits
of the regulation. Because the higher cost of compliance is experienced by everyone, the requirement does not violate the obligation to provide a reasonable accommodation or modification.

Note that the setback requirement in this example might be
a public regulation that is established by a zoning code, or it
might be a private regulation that is established by restrictive
covenants in a private subdivision. In some cases, public zoning and private covenants both may address setbacks. The key

distinction is that if the petitioner seeks an accommodation or modification of a zoning regulation, the request is to a zoning board of appeal and is evaluated under Title II of the ADA. If the request is for an exception to a private covenant, the request is to a HOA board and is covered by the FHA. Both the ADA and the FHA, as previously stated, use the same basic criteria and analysis.

The example of the ramp can be extended to any number of accommodations or modifications. When properly handled as a request for a reasonable accommodation to the regulations with respect to a ramp setback requirement, granting the exception is not technically a zoning variance and does not run with the land. The exception may be limited in duration for the benefit of the person for whom the accommodation or modification is made. The question of requiring restoration arises: can the petitioner, in our example, be required to restore the front entrance to her home—remove the ramp—when she leaves the property? This is important because restoration comes at a cost, and the requirement of restoration further increases the cost of adding the ramp. While cost alone usually is not a material factor, at least one court has cautioned that cost may be a significant factor if restoration costs are so high that they deter a petitioner from seeking a reasonable accommodation or modification for their disability.[149]

The third criterion is that the requested accommodation or modification must not fundamentally alter the program, service, or activity of the respondent, in the case of the ADA, or the rules, policies, practices, or services of the respondent, in the case of the FHA. What qualifies as a fundamental alteration

---

149. *See generally* Austin v. Town of Farmington, 826 F.3d 622 (2016).

is a difficult question, and it has not been clearly answered. We can suppose that a fundamental alteration has something to do with the inquiry of reasonableness under the criterion that the request be reasonable. By this, we mean that part of the inquiry should address the matter of whether the change produces an undue financial hardship or a substantial administrative burden for the respondent. It seems that a fundamental alteration is also something more than costs and burdens. In addition to addressing costs and burdens, the respondent should have to show that his requirements are pursuant to a rational plan, program, method, or business model, and that the requested change or exception fundamentally undermines the rationality of his planning or operating.

When a request for a reasonable accommodation or modification is presented to either a public entity or a private entity under an appropriate provision of the ADA, FHA, or RHA, it must be evaluated on the three stated criteria outlined here. Difficulty arises because many public and private boards, in the same context or proceedings, hear requests that are presented as an alternative to a standard variance or exception provided for in other rules, That is, the request is misinterpreted as being a standard request for a variance or exception covered by other local rules. When a petitioner's request raises a claim for a reasonable accommodation or modification, the decision maker must take evidence on and evaluate the request in the context of each of the three criteria under federal law. Ultimately, a decision about a request must be rational and supported by substantial competent evidence on the record. Given that the failure to provide a reasonable accommodation or modification is discrimination against a person with a disability, some people argue that the standard of review of a zoning board decision should have heightened scrutiny. The courts, however, have applied a rational basis standard when reviewing denials.

A question that remains in regard to rendering a proper decision is how the consideration of the three individual criteria are to be collectively considered and weighed. Must there be a finding in the affirmative for all three criteria? For example, must one find that the request is reasonable, necessary, *and* does not fundamentally alter to conclude that the denial of a request is actionable discrimination against a person protected by our federal disability laws? What if a request is determined to be reasonable on a cost and benefit basis and necessary, but it would fundamentally alter the plan, program, service, activity, and such of the respondent? Is concluding favorable to the petitioner on two out of three of the criteria sufficient?

Let's consider these questions in comparison to variances where we may have two different approaches. In New York, there is a five-factor balancing test for an area variance.[150] New York State also uses a four-factor test for a use variance, in which the petitioner must win on all four criteria.[151] In a balancing test, no single factor is determinative; a decision must be evaluated as rational in light of weighing and balancing the information going to each of the factors under consideration. In a collective or holistic sense, a decision is made on whether the balance is more or less favorable to the petitioner. This decision, of course, must be supported by rational reasons and justifications. The decision must be arrived at by applying the rules to the presence of substantial competent evidence on the record.

---

150. N.Y. Town Law § 267-b (3) (McKinney 2006). *See supra* note 123 for the five criteria of an area variance.

151. *Id.* at § 267-b (2). *See supra* note 124 for the four criteria of a use variance.

By contrast, in New York, with a request for a use variance, the petitioner will be denied the variance if the petitioner loses on any one of the four requirements.

What seems less than clear under our disability laws is whether we are to weigh all three of the criteria equally, balancing them collectively to make some sort of holistic determination, or whether we can safely conclude that an accommodation or modification is not required if any one of the criteria is inadequately supported by the evidence. The better view is that each request for a reasonable accommodation or modification should be evaluated on its own specific facts by using three specific criteria. In the end, a decision must be based on a holistic evaluation of these criteria in light of the totality of the evidence in the record.

This takes us back to the standard of review concerning discrimination against a person with a disability. Disability rights arise out of federal legislation and the prohibition against discrimination is statutorily defined. This is the reason that the standard of review is different and lower from that of situations involving classes of people determined by the Supreme Court to be in a suspect class. Generally, the standard of review in a case of discrimination involving a member of a suspect class is strict scrutiny. Strict scrutiny gives very little deference to an administrative decision. This is the case in a claim of racial discrimination. The denial of a request for a reasonable accommodation/modification is fundamentally different. Judicial review of these cases is on a rational basis standard. This standard of review provides significant deference to local administrative decisionmakers. A good starting point for further consideration of the matter involves considering how these claims arise. These claims typically arise out of requests for an exception or variance to some rule or procedure. In normal circumstances, if this type of request was made to a zoning board of appeal, for example, the standard of review for a quasi-judicial determination would be the rational basis standard supported by substantial competent evidence on the record. This is a higher standard than the fairly debatable standard of review applied to legislation. At the same time, it is not quite intermediate scrutiny nor is it strict scrutiny. Likewise, in a private HOA determination about a request for an exception or variance from governing rules and procedure, the standard of review generally is the business judgment rule. In each situation, however, a request for a reasonable accommodation or modification goes further than the ordinary request for a variance or exception. Under disability law, the decision-maker must elevate its review to consider whether the request is reasonable, whether it is necessary, and whether it will fundamentally alter the program, service, activity, rules, and procedures in question. This inquiry take us to a a higher level of investigation than the ordinary request for an exception or variance. Nonetheless, this does not rise to a higher standard of judicial review. Thus, it seems that, as to the determination of the three disability law criteria, the review is that a decision on the merits of each criterion must be rational and supported by substantial competent evidence on the record. While not without its critics, this has been the constitutional standard in cases involving disability since the decision in *City of Cleburne v. Cleburne Living Center, Inc.*, 473 U.S. 432 (1985).

8

Planning for Sidewalks

Sidewalks are critical pathways for navigating the many places in a community where life is lived out.[152] Sidewalks facilitate travel and enhance sustainability by reducing dependence on motor vehicles to travel within and among neighborhoods. Sidewalks also enhance public safety by providing pedestrians with a walking space outside of the roadway. People walking or moving in wheelchairs on public roadways can be dangerous, especially in the winter when snowbanks further block visibility and crowd the street. Sidewalks also provide locations for accessing public transit (such as bus stops) and offer protected crosswalks to assist in safely crossing busy roads.

There is no obligation under the Americans with Disabilities Act (ADA) for a local municipality to provide sidewalks. Consequently, a person with a disability cannot sue a local government for failure to have sidewalks. However, if sidewalks are

---

152. *See generally* MALLOY, *supra* note 6.

constructed, they must be fully compliant with the ADA. Once a walkway meets the definition of a sidewalk under a state or local highway law, local zoning code, or other regulation, it must be constructed and maintained in accordance with the provisions of the ADA, which sets forth certain design standards that allow sidewalks to be accessible to those confined to wheelchairs or those with otherwise limited mobility.[153] Retrofitting previously constructed sidewalks to meet the requirements of the ADA can be an expensive process and therefore, it is important to build sidewalks in compliance with the ADA in the first instance.

Generally speaking, state and local law, rather than federal law, governs building, locating, and funding sidewalks.[154] At the same time, if federal funds are used in the construction or alteration of a sidewalk, the Rehabilitation Act (RHA) and the ADA apply, even if the work is a state or local project.[155] In addition, many municipalities develop their own requirements for when sidewalks must be constructed. Often, municipalities require the construction of sidewalks as a condition of new development that shifts the cost burden of sidewalk construction from the municipality to the developer. In addition, municipal codes sometimes specifically address the requirements of the ADA by requiring structures, including sidewalks, to be ADA-compliant.

With respect to federal law, sidewalks must comply with the RHA and ADA when federal funds are used to support construction or alteration,[156] When sidewalks are newly constructed or

---

153. *See* 42 U.S.C. § 12101.

154. Although many sidewalks in New York are federally funded, the ADA places the burden of funding sidewalks on state and local entities.

155. Frame v. City of Arlington, 657 F.3d 215, 223 (5th Cir. 2011).

156. *See* Fed. High. Admin., *Questions and Answers About ADA Section 504*, https://www .fhwa.dot.gov/civilrights/programs/ada_sect504qa.cfm#q16 (last modified Oct. 25, 2018).

altered, they are considered facilities and pedestrian pathways.[157] Sidewalks also have been held to function as a program, service, or activity of state or local government, even when they do not receive federal funding.[158] In addition, the upkeep and maintenance of sidewalks are programs, services, or activities of state and local government.[159]

In *Barden v. City of Sacramento*,[160] the Ninth Circuit Court of Appeals held that "sidewalks are subject to program accessibility regulations promulgated in furtherance" of the ADA[161] and qualify as a "service, program or activity" within the meaning of Title II.[162] This means that sidewalks must be ADA-compliant, even if no federal funding is used to construct them. Nonetheless, in *Geiger v. City of Upper Arlington*,[163] the court referred to *Barden* and held that although sidewalk construction came under the ADA, communities were not required to build sidewalks. In other words, a city is not subject to a lawsuit by a person with a disability who asserts that the lack of sidewalks hinders her accessibility within the community. The city cannot be forced to build sidewalks.

In *Frame v. City of Arlington*,[164] the Fifth Circuit Court of Appeals held that both Title II of the ADA and Section 504 of the RHA apply to newly built and altered public sidewalks.[165] The Court reasoned that municipal authorities are "trustees for

---

157. 28 C.F.R. § 35.104; *see generally* Willits v. City of Los Angeles, 925 F. Supp. 2d 1089 (C.D. Cal. 2013).

158. Cohen v. City of Culver City, 754 F.3d 690, 695 (9th Cir. 2014).

159. Barden v. City of Sacramento, 292 F.3d 1073, 1077 (9th Cir. 2002).

160. *Id.* at 1073.

161. *Id.* at 1074.

162. *Id.* at 1076-77.

163. Geiger v. City of Upper Arlington, 2006 WL 1888877 (S.D. Ohio July 7, 2006).

164. *Frame*, 657 F.3d at 215.

165. *Id.* at 223.

the public" and "have [a] duty to keep [the] streets open and available for movement of people and property, the primary purpose to which streets are dedicated."[166] Consequently, when communities undertake to build sidewalks, they must make the sidewalks ADA-compliant because the sidewalks represent facilities as well as programs, services, and activities of the local government. They are facilities, programs, services, and activities that come under the ADA and RHA. The plaintiffs in *Frame* claimed that the city had sidewalks, but the inaccessibility of the sidewalks violated both Title II of the ADA and Section 504 of the RHA.[167] The Court agreed that the inaccessible sidewalks violated both Acts. The Court held that individuals, such as the plaintiffs, had a private right of action to enforce Title II of the ADA because sidewalks are "services, programs, or activities" of a public entity within the plain meaning of Title II.[168] Additionally, the court found that sidewalks qualified as a "program or activity" under the RHA because this definition included "all of the operations of . . . a local government."[169] As to the RHA, the Court also considered the fact that federal funding was used to build or alter the sidewalks, and this brought the sidewalks under the RHA.[170]

New construction and the alteration of sidewalks require compliance with the ADA to the maximum extent possible. The only defense to noncompliance is structural impracticability. This standard is very high, and is difficult to prove. Proof of structural impracticability generally requires a showing of unique

166. Schneider v. New Jersey, 308 U.S. 147, 160 (1939).

167. *See Frame*, 657 F.3d at 221.

168. *Id*. at 227.

169. *Id*. at 225 (quoting 29 U.S.C. § 794(B)(1)(A)).

170. *Id*.

characteristics that make the attainment of full accessibility unduly difficult. Importantly, structural impracticability cannot be demonstrated by simply presenting evidence of a high cost to comply. Under case decisions, the courts have held that the RHA makes structural impracticability the only defense when considering the accessibility of new construction and alterations, and the ADA is to be interpreted the same as the RHA in this regard.[171]

While many of the case decisions that deal with sidewalks address sidewalks as programs, services, and activities of local government, there are cases that clearly identify sidewalks as also being facilities. *Willits v. City of Los Angeles* is one such case.[172] In *Willits*, plaintiffs sued the city under the ADA and the RHA alleging that the city was failing in its obligation to properly install and maintain sidewalks. The court classified sidewalks both as facilities *and* as programs, services, and activities of local government. The court then held that all new construction and alterations of sidewalks had to be accessible to the maximum extent possible, and that the only defense under both the RHA and the ADA is structural impracticability.[173] The court specifically rejected the defense of undue financial or administrative burden.[174]

The issue of building new sidewalks is relatively easy to identify; the more difficult questions arise in determining whether the sidewalk is altered when a community considers making repairs or improvements to sidewalks and streets. Title 28 C.F.R. § 35.150(a)

---

171. *Willits*, 925 F. Supp. 2d at 1093 (noting that cities may not put forth an "undue financial burden" defense for new construction and alterations).

172. *Id.*

173. 28 C.F.R. § 35.151.

174. *Willits*, 925 F. Supp. 2d at 1093.

states that public entities must operate services, programs, or activities so that each, when viewed in its entirety, is readily accessible to and usable by individuals with disabilities.[175] Given that the focus is on viewing services, programs, and activities in their "entirety," it probably is not required that a community have every aspect and every foot of its sidewalk system ADA-complaint. Older sidewalks are required to be updated to the extent that updating does not impose an undue administrative or financial burden.[176] Additionally, when considered as a sidewalk system, less than full compliance across the system may be permitted based on constraints of prior construction (such as historic buildings positioned with little or no room for sidewalks between them and the street), or because of the topography of the landscape. There also are limits that are acceptable in situations where places of historical significance may be affected. The general requirements of disability law impose a duty on local governments to make facilities, programs, services, and activities accessible to people with disabilities, but there are some exceptions. An example is when a local government demonstrates that updating every aspect of its existing sidewalk system to be fully ADA-compliant imposes an undue administrative or financial burden. Here, as with the defense of structural impracticability for alterations and new construction, the local government that asserts an exception to compliance has the burden of making the case to support the asserted exception. Evidence in support of the exception might include engineering reports, a cost analysis,

---

175. 28 C.F.R. § 35.150(a).

176. *Willits*, 925 F. Supp. 2d at 1094 (explaining that "Title II of the ADA provides an undue financial burden defense for facilities already in existence as of January 26, 1992, but not for facilities constructed or altered after that date. 28 C.F.R. § 35.150. The Rehabilitation Act provides similarly for facilities constructed or altered after June 3, 1977.").

and an explanation of the undue administrative and financial burden. With respect to sidewalks, some stretches of sidewalk may need updating more than others, and updating may cost much more in one location than in others. This fact on its own does not make for an undue burden. The issue of an undue burden is not only about the cost of a component, part, or particular stretch of a sidewalk; it should be about the cost relative to the local government's finances, tax base, and other factors. The cost of sidewalk upkeep in one small location ought to be considered relative to the expenditure on overall sidewalk projects and with respect to the locations and places being connected by this pathway (such as public buildings).

When building a new road, adjoining sidewalks typically are considered part of the system, and they must comply with the ADA and RHA. Short of new road construction, roads often are resurfaced or upgraded. One key issue when resurfacing or upgrading streets is whether or not the work amounts to an alteration to the road. If it is considered an alteration, the community will have to make all sidewalks along the roadway compliant with the ADA and the RHA to the maximum extent possible. This issue was addressed in *Kinney v. Yerusalim*,[177] wherein the plaintiffs argued that resurfacing a street constituted an "alteration" under section 35.151(i), and the city was, therefore, required to provide curb ramps or slopes on all streets that had been resurfaced since January 26, 1992, the effective date of the statute. The city argued that resurfacing was not an activity that rose to the level of an alteration under the statute, and that the city was not required to install curb ramps

---

177. Kinney v. Yerusalim, 812 F. Supp. 547 (E.D. Pa. 1993).

or slopes.[178] The court rejected the city's argument. The court cited the ADA Accessibility Guidelines (ADAAG) and held that Title II of the ADA is triggered whenever an alteration "affects or could affect the usability of [the] facility."[179] The court discussed the definition of "usability" and concluded that the term should "be read broadly to include any change that affects the usability of the facility, not simply changes that relate directly to access by individuals with disabilities."[180] Thus, "[w]hether resurfacing a street constitutes an 'alteration'" depends on "whether resurfacing affects the usability of the street."[181] The court concluded that resurfacing a street made it more usable, and that resurfacing constituted an "alteration" under the ADA. Thus, the city was required to construct curb ramps on all streets that had been resurfaced after January 26, 1992.[182] Note that in this case, the court also refers to a sidewalk and street as "facilities." Thus, one must be careful in this area, because sidewalks can come within the terms both of "facilities" and of "programs, services, and activities."

Alterations go beyond normal maintenance of roads or sidewalks. Alterations require sidewalks to be ADA-compliant, but not everything is an alteration. Likewise, alterations to a roadway may trigger a requirement to upgrade adjoining sidewalks. The difficult question is one of determining when roadwork becomes something more than normal upkeep and is treated as an alteration. We can get some assistance on answering this question by referring to the Federal Highway Administration

---

178. *Id.* at 549.

179. *Id.* (quoting 28 C.F.R. § 35.151(b) (2015)) (omitting emphasis on "usability").

180. *Id.* at 551 (quoting 28 C.F.R. Pt. 36, App. C (2015)).

181. *Id.* at 551.

182. *Id.* at 552.

(FHWA). The FHWA defines "maintenance activities" as "actions that are intended to preserve the system, retard future deterioration, and maintain the functional condition of the roadway without increasing the structural capacity."[183] We also can get guidance from the Department of Justice (DOJ). The DOJ has stated that the following maintenance activities are *not* considered alterations: filling potholes, joint repair, pavement patching, shoulder repair, striping, signing, and draining system repairs.[184] However, the following projects are considered alterations by the DOJ: resurfacing beyond normal maintenance, reconstruction, rehabilitation, widening, and traffic signal installation.

Under the ADA, municipalities are responsible for the general upkeep of sidewalks to ensure that they remain open and usable to persons with disabilities.[185] This general upkeep includes but is not limited to snow and debris removal, maintaining an accessible path throughout work zones, and corrections of any other disruptions.[186] Cities and villages are responsible for the upkeep of state-constructed roads within city boundaries.[187] Sidewalk alteration and construction must comply with accessible design standards to the maximum extent possible. The only defense is structural impracticability. The maintenance of sidewalks and removal of snow from sidewalks would be a program, service, or

---

183. Fed. High. Admin., *supra* note 156, at q. 18.

184. *See* FED. HIGH. ADMIN., DEP'T OF JUSTICE/DEP'T OF TRANSP., JOINT TECHNICAL ASSISTANCE ON THE TITLE II OF THE AMERICANS WITH DISABILITIES ACT REQUIREMENTS TO PROVIDE CURB RAMPS WHEN STREETS, ROADS, OR HIGHWAYS ARE ALTERED THROUGH RESURFACING (2013), http://www.fhwa.dot.gov/civilrights/programs/doj_fhwa_ta.cfm.

185. *See* 28 C.F.R. § 35.133 (2015). *See also* Fed. High. Admin., *supra* note 157.

186. *See* UNITED STATES ACCESS BOARD, ADA ACCESSIBILITY GUIDELINES § 4.1.1(4) (2010), https://www.access-board.gov/guidelines-and-standards/buildings-and-sites/about-the-ada-standards/ada-standards [*hereinafter*, ADAAG].

187. *See* N.Y. HIGH. LAW §§ 46 & 349-C (McKinney).

activity of local government. For this, compliance must be to the maximum extent possible, with an available defense of undue financial or administrative burden. This is a high standard, but it is not as high as the standard of proof required to demonstrate structural impracticability.

Under the ADA, Title II, Subpart B, "[a] public entity shall maintain in operable working condition those features of facilities and equipment that are required to be readily accessible to and usable by persons with disabilities by the Act or this part."[188] This requirement does not apply to "temporary interruptions in service or access due to maintenance or repairs."[189] Therefore, if a community is seeking to comply with the ADA, the fact that there is a temporary disruption in a facility, service, program, or activity may not make the community liable for violation of our disability laws.

When considering the building of sidewalks and other pedestrian pathways, it is important to know that it is not sufficient to simply provide "accessible routes" if the routes are not maintained in a manner that enables individuals with disabilities to use them. Specifically, if the route is obstructed so that it is neither "accessible to" nor "usable by" individuals with disabilities, it is noncompliant.[190] In 2010, the DOJ released the latest official guidelines for accessible design.[191] These guidelines require that at least one accessible route must be provided on "public streets and sidewalks; and public transportation stops

---

188. 28 C.F.R § 35.133(a) (2015).

189. *Id.* § 35.133(b).

190. *See* KATHY E. HINCK ET AL., AM. JUR. 2D *Americans with Disabilities Act Analysis and Implications* § 279 (2015).

191. *See* U.S. DEP'T OF JUSTICE, 2010 ADA STANDARDS FOR ACCESSIBLE DESIGN (2010), https://www.ada.gov/regs2010/2010ADAStandards/2010ADAstandards.htm.

to the accessible building or facility entrance they serve," with exceptions for historic buildings and vehicle-only paths.[192]

In 2011, the United States Access Board (USAB) released proposed guidelines for adoption of "accessibility standards in regulations issued by other federal agencies implementing Title II of the Americans with Disabilities Act."[193] Under the proposed guidelines, pedestrian access routes must be provided in these locations:

- Sidewalks and other pedestrian circulation paths located in the public right-of-way
- Pedestrian street crossings and at-grade rail crossings, including medians and pedestrian refuge islands
- Overpasses, underpasses, bridges, and similar structures that contain pedestrian circulation paths[194]

In an FHWA memorandum titled *Snow Removal on Sidewalks Constructed with Federal Funding*, snow and ice removal from sidewalks is considered a pedestrian accessibility issue.[195] Public agencies must keep sidewalks and walkways accessible to people with disabilities. Only temporary interruptions are permitted.[196] This obligation includes reasonable snow removal

---

192. *Id.* § 206.2.1.

193. See UNITED STATES ACCESS BOARD, SECTION-BY-SECTION ANALYSIS, *in* PROPOSED GUIDELINES FOR PEDESTRIAN FACILITIES IN THE PUBLIC RIGHT-OF-WAY (published in the Federal Register on July 26, 2011; 36 C.F.R. Part 1190 Docket No. ATBCB 2011-04), https://www.access-board.gov/guidelines-and-standards/streets-sidewalks/public-rights-of-way/proposed-rights-of-way-guidelines/section-by-section-analysis (last visited Sept. 29, 2019).

194. *Id.*

195. *See* U.S. Dep't of Transp. & Fed. High. Admin., Mem. from Batch Wlaschin to Dirs. of Field Servs. and Div. Adm'rs, *Information: Snow Removal on Sidewalks Constructed with Federal Funding* (Aug. 27, 2008), http://www.fhwa.dot.gov/preservation/082708.cfm.

196. *Id.*

efforts.[197] While there is a recognition that snow conditions vary among the states, local governments are required to develop policies that provide for the removal of snow and ice from "their own roadways and adjoining pedestrian facilities."[198]

More specifically, the ADA requires public entities with more than 50 employees to establish transition plans for sidewalk accessibility.[199] The transition plan is intended to identify system needs and integrate them with the state's planning process. The schedule should first provide for pedestrian access upgrades to "[s]tate and local government offices and facilities, transportation, places of public accommodation, and employers, followed by walkways serving other areas."[200] Each transition plan should accomplish four tasks:

1. Identify physical obstacles in the public entity's facilities that limit the accessibility of its programs or activities to individuals with disabilities.
2. Describe in detail the methods that will be used to make the facilities accessible.
3. Specify the schedule for taking the steps necessary to upgrade pedestrian access to meet ADA and Section 504 requirements in each year following the transition plan.
4. Indicate the official who is responsible for implementation of the plan.[201]

---

197. *Id.*
198. *Id.*
199. *See* 28 C.F.R. § 35.150(d)(1) (2015).
200. *Id.*
201. *Id.* § 35.150(d)(3).

In addition to this planning requirement, local communities must also comply with the requirements for "Olmstead planning," as discussed earlier in this book.

In planning and executing an accessible sidewalk plan, guidance addressing ramping, curb cutting, width and turning radius requirements, as well as the placement of benches, signs, and bus stops[202] is offered from several sources, including the DOJ;[203] the U.S. Department of Transportation;[204] the USAB;[205] and state governments.[206]

The following chart outlines the basic standards that are applicable to sidewalks as discussed in this chapter:

Activity	Accessibility	Defense to Compliance
New Construction and Alteration	Maximum Extent Possible	Structural Impracticability
Maintenance and Snow Removal	Maximum Extent Possible	Undue Financial or Administrative Burden
Updating Existing, Older Sidewalks	Maximum Extent Possible	Undue Financial or Administrative Burden

202. *See* UNITED STATES ACCESS BOARD, ADA ACCESSIBILITY GUIDELINES (2002), *supra* note 40.

203. *See* U.S. DEP'T OF JUSTICE, GUIDANCE ON THE 2010 ADA STANDARDS FOR ACCESSIBLE DESIGN, https://www.ada.gov/regs2010/2010ADAStandards/Guidance_2010ADAStandards .pdf.

204. *See* U.S. DEP'T OF TRANSP., DESIGNING PEDESTRIAN FACILITIES FOR ACCESSIBILITY, http://dot .state.nm.us/content/dam/nmdot/OEOP/ADA_Module-3.pdf.

205. *See, e.g.*, ADAAG, *supra* note 186. In addition to dealing with issues of snow removal, communities should inventory the extent to which existing pathways fail to meet ADA requirements. These communities must also make sure that new and altered sidewalks comply with the ADA. Communities also must affirmatively plan for constructing and financing upgrades to existing sidewalks so that all pathways will be fully accessible to all residents without regard to disability.

206. *See* U.S. DEP'T OF JUSTICE, *supra* note 191; N.Y. STATE DEP'T OF TRANSP., HIGHWAY DESIGN MANUAL, https://www.dot.ny.gov/divisions/engineering/design/dqab/hdm/hdm -repository/chapt_18.pdf.

This chart applies to public facilities and structures. As a point of reference, consider the obligation to update noncompliant existing facilities that are privately owned places of public accommodation. Here, the standard is one of making changes and updates to the extent that greater accessibility is "readily achievable."[207] This is discussed in more detail in chapter 12, which addresses additional concerns under Title III of the ADA.

---

207. *See generally* Colorado Cross Disability Coal. v. Hermanson Fam. Ltd. Partn. I, 264 F.3d 999, 1005 (10th Cir. 2001).

9

Emotional Support and Service Animals

There is a lot of confusion surrounding service animals and emotional support animals. To begin with, the Americans with Disabilities Act (ADA) has a different meaning for service animal than does the Fair Housing Act (FHA) and the Rehabilitation Act (RHA). Under the ADA, a service animal refers only to a dog or a miniature horse. There are also training requirements under the ADA, and service animals are not considered to be pets. The FHA and RHA definition of service animal includes many other animals. These animals may be pets or emotional support animals as well as service animals under the definition applied in the ADA. Unfortunately, the FHA and RHA use the same term as the ADA, "service animal." Under the ADA service animals are permitted wherever their owner is permitted. In contrast, an emotional support animal is permitted on the basis of a reasonable accommodation. In this chapter keep in mind

101

that "service animal" under the ADA is not the same as "service animal" under the FHA and RHA.

The FHA and Section 504 of the RHA differ from the ADA in terms of when a reasonable accommodation and reasonable modification need to be granted for different service (emotional support) animals. The reasonable accommodation provisions of the FHA and Section 504 of the RHA arise when a qualified individual with a disability uses or wants to use a service (emotional support) animal in housing where the provider precludes residents from having pets or has pet restrictions.[208] Under the FHA and RHA, service animals include pets but a service animal as defined under the ADA is not considered a pet.[209]

Under both the FHA and Section 504, it is not necessary for service (emotional support) animals to be trained.[210] Under the ADA, they must be trained. Dogs are the most common animals used as service animals, but other animals can be used.[211] Service animals are animals that provide assistance and/or emotional support for an individual with a disability. The functions provided by service animals can include guiding blind individuals, alerting deaf individuals of a sound, getting items, and alerting to an impending seizure.

There are two questions a housing provider must consider after receiving a request for a reasonable accommodation: "(1) does the person seeking to use and live with the animal have a disability; and (2) does the person making the request have a disability-related need for an assistance animal?"[212]

---

208. U.S. Dep't of Hous. & Urban Dev., FHEO Notice FHEO-2013-01 (Apr. 25, 2013), https://archives.hud.gov/news/2013/servanimals_ntcfheo2013-01.pdf.
209. *Id.*
210. *Id.*
211. *Id.*
212. *Id.*

If the answer to either of these questions is no, the request for the reasonable accommodation may be denied. Remember that under the FHA, a service animal includes animals that provide emotional support, and in this regard, it differs from the ADA.

If the answer to both of the above questions is yes, the FHA and Section 504 require the housing provider to make a reasonable accommodation. This means that the housing provider is required to modify the no-pets policy to allow the person with the disability to use a service animal in all areas of the premises where persons are normally permitted to go, unless allowing this modification would create an undue hardship.[213] Moreover, the housing provider is prohibited from charging the tenant with a service animal an additional fee, although the housing provider can charge for reasonable and expected wear and tear from the animal.[214]

A housing provider also is allowed to deny a request for a reasonable accommodation or modification if the specific service animal imposes a direct threat to the safety and health of others or if the specific service animal would cause physical damage to the property that cannot be eliminated by another reasonable accommodation.[215] However, the housing provider is not allowed to place standards for breed, size, or weight on service animals.[216] Finding that a specific service animal imposes a direct threat or that it could cause physical damage requires the housing provider to make an individualized assessment based on objective evidence. A decision based on speculation is not

---

213. *Id.*

214. *Id.* at fn. 6. *See also* Baughman v. City of Elkhart, 2018 U.S. Dist. LEXIS 50241 (E.D. Tex. 2018). (A woman was denied an accommodation for her emotional support animal, which was a pet lemur. Denial was deemed reasonable because the pet was a threat to public safety.)

215. *Id.*

216. *Id.*

sufficient to deny the requested reasonable accommodation.[217] Additionally, conditions and restrictions that housing providers apply to pets cannot be applied to service animals (i.e., housing providers cannot charge a pet deposit for a service animal).[218]

However, different rules may apply simultaneously or separately to a housing provider under the ADA regarding service animals. The ADA regulations define service animal as:

> . . . any dog that is individually trained to do work or perform tasks for the benefit of an individual with a disability, including a physical, sensory, psychiatric, intellectual, or other mental disability. Other species of animals, whether wild or domestic, trained or untrained, are not service animals for the purposes of this definition.[219]

This is a narrow definition that defines only trained dogs as service animals. Furthermore, emotional support animals are precluded under this definition. Recently, miniature horses have been included as service animals.[220] The different definition of service animals in the ADA compared to the FHA and Section 504 of the RHA require the determination of whether a service animal is permitted to be handled as a definitional analysis and not under the reasonable accommodation analysis.[221]

If it is not readily apparent that the service animal is trained to perform tasks for the individual with the disability, the person seeking to deny the presence of the animal (the covered entity)

---

217. *Id.*

218. *Id.*

219. 28 C.F.R. § 35.104.

220. 28 C.F.R. 36.104; 28 C.F.R. § 35.136 - Service animals.

221. U.S. Dep't of Hous. & Urban Dev., *supra* note 208.

can ask two questions in its analysis of whether the service animal is permitted: "(1) is this a service animal that is required because of a disability?; and (2) what work or tasks has the animal been trained to perform?"[222] A covered entity under the ADA cannot ask for documentation regarding the certification of the service animal.[223] If the service animal satisfies the above conditions, then it is permitted to be in all areas of the facility where any member of the public can be.[224]

A service animal that satisfies the above two questions can be denied access to a covered entity under the ADA if the animal is out of control and the owner cannot control it, if the animal is not housebroken, or if the animal poses a direct threat to the health and safety of others.[225] Similar to finding a direct threat under the FHA and Section 504 of the RHA, under the ADA, finding a direct threat requires an individualized assessment that cannot be based on stereotypes.[226]

The reasonable accommodation requirement under Section 504 of the RHA is similar to that in the FHA, but Section 504 applies only to programs and activities that receive federal funds. The FHA also has a broader application.[227]

In the context of housing, the FHA applies to zoning to the extent that it requires zoning officials to make reasonable exceptions to policies and practices to afford people with disabilities an equal opportunity to obtain housing.[228]

---

222. *Id.*
223. *Id.*
224. *Id.*
225. *Id.*
226. *Id.*
227. Malloy, *supra* note 1, at 113. *See* 29 U.S.C. § 794 (2006) *and* 42 U.S.C. § 3601 (2006).
228. 42 U.S.C. § 3601.

To summarize, service animals under the ADA are not pets and are permitted to go wherever the public can go. Under the FHA and RHA, service animals include emotional support animals, including pets, and are permitted in places based on the criteria for providing a reasonable accommodation or modification.

The guidelines on service animals are set out in 28 C.F.R. § 35.136 and are provided here:

§ 35.136 Service animals.

(a) *General.* Generally, a public entity shall modify its policies, practices, or procedures to permit the use of a service animal by an individual with a disability.

(b) *Exceptions.* A public entity may ask an individual with a disability to remove a service animal from the premises if -

(1) The animal is out of control and the animal's handler does not take effective action to control it; or

(2) The animal is not housebroken.

(c) *If an animal is properly excluded.* If a public entity properly excludes a service animal under § 35.136(b), it shall give the individual with a disability the opportunity to participate in the service, program, or activity without having the service animal on the premises.

(d) *Animal under handler's control.* A service animal shall be under the control of its handler. A service animal shall have a harness, leash, or other tether, unless either the handler is unable because of a disability to use a harness, leash, or other tether, or the use of a harness, leash, or other tether would interfere with the service animal's safe, effective performance of work or tasks, in which case the service animal must be otherwise under the handler's control (*e.g.*, voice control, signals, or other effective means).

(e) *Care or supervision.* A public entity is not responsible for the care or supervision of a service animal.

(f) *Inquiries.* A public entity shall not ask about the nature or extent of a person's disability, but may make two inquiries to determine whether an animal qualifies as a service animal. A public entity may ask if the animal is required because of a disability and what work or task the animal has been trained to perform. A public entity shall not require documentation, such as proof that the animal has been certified, trained, or licensed as a service animal. Generally, a public entity may not make these inquiries about a service animal when it is readily apparent that an animal is trained to do work or perform tasks for an individual with a disability (*e.g.*, the dog is observed guiding an individual who is blind or has low vision, pulling a person's wheelchair, or providing assistance with stability or balance to an individual with an observable mobility disability).

(g) *Access to areas of a public entity.* Individuals with disabilities shall be permitted to be accompanied by their service animals in all areas of a public entity's facilities where members of the public, participants in services, programs or activities, or invitees, as relevant, are allowed to go.

(h) *Surcharges.* A public entity shall not ask or require an individual with a disability to pay a surcharge, even if people accompanied by pets are required to pay fees, or to comply with other requirements generally not applicable to people without pets. If a public entity normally charges individuals for the damage they cause, an individual with a disability may be charged for damage caused by his or her service animal.

(i) *Miniature horses.*

(1) *Reasonable modifications.* A public entity shall make reasonable modifications in policies, practices, or procedures to permit the use of a miniature horse by an individual with a disability if the miniature horse has been individually trained to do work or perform tasks for the benefit of the individual with a disability.

(2) *Assessment factors.* In determining whether reasonable modifications in policies, practices, or procedures can be made to allow a miniature horse into a specific facility, a public entity shall consider -

(i) The type, size, and weight of the miniature horse and whether the facility can accommodate these features;

(ii) Whether the handler has sufficient control of the miniature horse;

(iii) Whether the miniature horse is housebroken; and

(iv) Whether the miniature horse's presence in a specific facility compromises legitimate safety requirements that are necessary for safe operation.

(3) *Other requirements.* Paragraphs 35.136(c) through (h) of this section, which apply to service animals, shall also apply to miniature horses.

10

Standing

In this chapter, we consider the qualifications for standing under each of the three primary federal Acts that govern federal disability law.

ADA

To establish standing to bring a case in court under the Americans with Disabilities Act (ADA), a plaintiff must show an injury in fact that meets the following three requirements: (1) concrete and particularized or an actual and imminent injury that is not hypothetical; (2) the injury is fairly traceable to a challenged action of the defendant; and (3) the injury is likely to be redressed by a favorable decision.[229]

---

229. Transport Workers Union of America v. New York City Transit Authority, 342 F. Supp. 2d 160, 165-67 (S.D. N.Y. 2004); Ross v. City of Gatlinburg, Tenn., 327 F. Supp. 2d 834, 841-43 (E.D. Tenn. 2003).

There has been disagreement as to whether the U.S. Attorney General has standing to bring suit under Title II of the ADA.[230] The court in *C.V. v. Dudek* stated that the enforcement provision in Title II was distinct from the enforcement provisions in Title I and Title III.[231] Under Title I and Title III, the enforcement provision directly confers standing on the Attorney General.[232] Whereas, Title II grants standing to "persons alleging discrimination," the Attorney General is not considered a person under this title.[233] The court reached its conclusion by saying; "Where Congress has conferred standing on a particular actor in one section of a statutory scheme, but not in another, its silence must be read to preclude standing."[234] This decision has since been overruled by the decision of the U.S. Court of Appeals for the 11th Circuit, which held that the U.S. Attorney General does have standing to bring a suit under Title II.[235]

The Department of Justice (DOJ) also has been allowed to intervene on a pending Title II suit.[236] In *Steward v. Abbott*, the Attorney General was allowed to intervene and was not required to show standing because the Attorney General sought no more relief beyond what the plaintiffs sought.[237]

There is no specific statute of limitations under the ADA. Typically, the state statute of limitations that is most analogous to the plaintiff's claim governs.

---

230. C.V. v. Dudek, 209 F. Supp. 3d 1279, 1282 (S.D. Fla. 2016).

231. *Id.*

232. *Id.* at 1282-83 (citing 42 United States Code (U.S.C.) § 12188(b)(1)(B); 41 U.S.C. § 12117(a)).

233. *Id.* at 1284.

234. *Id.* at 1283.

235. U.S. v. Fla., 2019 WL 4439465 (11th Cir. Sept. 17, 2019). This case involved the consolidation of several cases on appeal, including *C.V. v. Dudek*, 209 F. Supp. 3d 1279, 1282.

236. Steward v. Abbott, 189 F. Supp. 3d 620, 624-27 (W.D. Tex. 2016).

237. *Id.* at 625.

SECTION 504 OF THE RHA

The general rule is that an individual who is not disabled within the terms of the Rehabilitation Act (RHA) lacks standing to sue under Section 504 of that Act. However, a group of disabled persons that form an organization traditionally have standing to sue if the group can establish a sufficient nexus between the organization and the injury claimed. For a plaintiff seeking injunctive relief to have standing under Section 504, the plaintiff must show a real or immediate threat of future injury.[238] Some courts have seemed to lessen the burden required for a plaintiff to establish standing. For example, some courts have found standing where the injury occurred in the past, but it is illustrated that the lack of accommodation still exists.

Section 504 does not require that administrative remedies be exhausted against a federal grantee. This means that the statute of limitations runs while administrative remedies are being brought. The relevant statute of limitations that governs Section 504 claims are the relevant state's limitations for personal injury actions.[239]

Third-Party Standing

Quoting from the opinion in *RHJ Medical Center, Inc. v. City of DuBois*,[240] the ADA and RHA grant third-party standing under these conditions:

> Generally, a "plaintiff . . . must assert his own legal rights and interests and cannot rest his claim to relief on the legal rights or interests of third parties." However,

---

238. Davis v. Flexman, 109 F. Supp. 2d 776 (S.D. Ohio, 1999); Schroedel v. N.Y. Univ. Med. Ctr., 995 F. Supp. 594 (S.D.N.Y., 1995).

239. Holmes v. Tex. A&M Univ., 145 F.3d 681 (5th Cir. 1998) (citing 42 U.S.C. § 1988(a)).

240. RHJ Med. Cntr., Inc. v. City of DuBois, 754 F. Supp. 2d 723 (W.D. Pa. 2010).

"Congress may grant an express right of action to persons who otherwise would be barred by prudential standing rules." In certain cases, standing may exist because of statutorily created rights: "[T]he standing question in such cases is whether the constitutional or statutory provision on which the claim rests properly can be understood as granting persons in the plaintiff's position a right to judicial relief." Where Congress grants a right of action to an entity or association, the entity may assert standing either in its own right or on behalf of its members. . . .[241]

The ADA and RHA are statutes in which Congress has granted third party standing. The regulation implementing Title II of the ADA provides, "A public entity shall not exclude or otherwise deny equal services, programs, or activities to an individual or entity because of the known disability of an individual with whom the individual or entity is known to *have a relationship or association*." 28 C.F.R. § 35.130(g) (emphasis added). This provision establishes the basis for associational standing. The "prudential limits imposed in pure associational standing cases do not apply to" statutory grants of associational standing. This broad conception of standing does indeed "extend standing to the full limits of Article III." So "long as this requirement [of Article III] is satisfied, persons to whom Congress has granted a right of action, either expressly or by clear implication, may have standing to seek relief on the basis of the legal rights and interests of others, and

---

indeed, may invoke the general public interest in support of their claim."[242]

FHA

Standing under the Fair Housing Act (FHA) is satisfied by minimum constitutional case or controversy requirements of Article III.[243] This requires: (1) actual or threatened injury; (2) injury that is caused by or is fairly traceable to defendant's challenged action; and (3) injury that is likely to be redressed by a favorable court decision.[244]

Under the FHA, the language of the statute permits any "aggrieved person" or the U.S. Attorney General to bring a lawsuit to enforce the FHA. The FHA defines an aggrieved person as "any person who (1) claims to have been injured by a discriminatory housing practice; or (2) believes that such person will be injured by a discriminatory housing practice that is about to occur."[245] The court has found that there was a congressional intention to define *aggrieved person* as broadly as possible.[246]

An aggrieved person may commence a civil action in an appropriate United States District Court or State court no later than two years after the occurrence or the termination of an alleged discriminatory housing practice.[247]

---

242. *Id*. (citation omitted).

243. *See* 42 U.S.C. § 3610(1)(A)(i);. 42 U.S.C. § 3602(i); Trafficante v. Metropolitan Life Ins. Co., 409 U.S. 205, 209 (1972); Hallmark Devs., Inc. v. Fulton Cty., Georgia, 386 F. Supp. 2d 1369, 1381 (N.D. Ga. 2005).

244. *Hallmark Developers*, 386 F. Supp. 2d at 1381.

245. 42 U.S.C. § 3602(i).

246. *Id*.; *Trafficante*, 409 U.S. at 209.

247. 42 U.S.C. § 3613(a)(1)(A) (2016).

A recent U.S. Supreme Court decision held that cities may be aggrieved persons under the FHA, following the congressional intent to confer standing broadly.[248]

In another case, developers who sought to build low-income housing had standing under the FHA to challenge a county's denial of a rezoning request.[249] The developers were able to show that they had been injured by the denial and that there was a disparate impact upon minority residents that was discriminatory.[250]

248. Bank of America v. City of Miami, Fla., 137 S.Ct. 1296, 1303 (2017).
249. *Hallmark Devs.*, 386 F. Supp. 2d at 1381.
250. *Id.*

11

Remedies

The Americans with Disabilities Act (ADA), the Fair Housing Act (FHA), and the Rehabilitation Act (RHA) offer remedies for violation of their requirements. "An action based on an allegation of discrimination under the ADA, FHA, and RHA may be pursuant to one or more of the three theories set out earlier: intentional discrimination (disparate treatment), disparate impact, and failure to make a reasonable modification."[251]

A Title II claim under the ADA "may be established by evidence that (1) the defendant intentionally acted on the basis of the disability, (2) the defendant refused to provide a reasonable modification, or (3) the defendant's rule disproportionately impacts disabled people."[252] Title II adopts the remedies available under the RHA in 42 United States Code (U.S.C.) § 12133, which in turn adopts the remedies of the Civil Rights Act of

---

251. MALLOY, *supra* note 1, at 143. (Reasonable modification includes accommodation.)
252. *Wis. Cmty. Servs.*, 465 F.3d 737 at 753.

1964 as detailed in 29 U.S.C. § 794a(a)(2). Compensatory damages are available if a plaintiff shows that the discrimination by the public entity was intentional, defined as deliberate indifference to an individual's rights, or actual malice.[253] Injunctive relief also is available under Title II.[254] Punitive damages are not available, though, no matter how deliberate and malicious the conduct.[255] Per 28 Code of Federal Regulations (C.F.R.) § 35.175, attorney fees and court cost awards are at the discretion of the court.

If one brings a suit against a state for violating federal disability law, state government entities may assert immunity under the 11th Amendment to the U.S. Constitution. Depending on the violation, the state may be immune to damages.[256]

Under Title III of the ADA, private parties may seek remedies under 42 U.S.C. § 2000a-3(a). Private parties may receive equitable relief, but they cannot be awarded damages as a result of their ADA Title III lawsuit.[257] However, courts may award reasonable attorney fees if the private party wins the lawsuit, including court costs.[258]

In cases brought by the Department of Justice (DOJ), the court may award compensatory damages, civil penalties, attorney fees, and court costs as detailed in 28 C.F.R. § 36.504.

Under the ADA, a plaintiff or the representative of a plaintiff can choose to file an administrative complaint. The administrative complaint process is governed by the regulations in

---

253. Duvall v. County of Kitsap, 260 F.3d 1124 (9th Cir. 2001).

254. Fortyune v. American Multi-Cinema, Inc., 364 F.3d 1075 (9th Cir. 2004).

255. Barnes v. Gorman, 536 U.S. 181 (2002).

256. *See* Tennessee v. Lane, 541 U.S. 509 (2004).

257. Goodwin v. C.J.N., Inc., 436 F.3d 44, 50 (1st Cir. 2006).

258. *See* 42 U.S.C. § 2000a-3(b).

28 C.F.R. §§ 35.170-35.174. An appropriate federal agency is either the designated agency under Subpart G of the regulations or any agency that provides funding to the public entity. An individual also could file an administrative complaint with the DOJ, which would refer the complaint to the proper agency. An individual is not required to file a grievance directly with the public entity that committed the discrimination as a prerequisite to filing any administrative complaint.

After receiving the complaint, the federal agency issues either a "letter of findings" or resolves the complaint. Resolving the complaint should include an attempt to negotiate a voluntary agreement with the public agency.[259] If the federal agency is unable to reach a resolution, the agency is required to refer the complaint to the DOJ for further action.

However, it is not necessary for a plaintiff to exhaust administrative remedies before filing a cause of action against a public entity with the federal court.[260]

Section 504 of the RHA adopts the remedies that are available under Title VI of the Civil Rights Act of 1964.[261] Therefore, compensatory damages and injunctive relief are available and punitive damages are unavailable under 42 U.S.C § 2000d-7. Reasonable attorney fees also may be awarded.

The FHA provides several remedies. The DOJ, the Department of Housing and Urban Development (HUD), and private parties all may bring suit to enforce the FHA's anti-discrimination

---

259. RUTH COLKER, FEDERAL DISABILITY LAW IN A NUTSHELL 209 (2015).

260. Bledsoe v. Palm Beach Cty. Soil & Water Conserv. Dist., 133 F.3d 816, 824 (11th Cir. 1998); see e.g., Bogovich v. Sandoval, 189 F.3d 999 (9th Cir. 1999).

261. 29 U.S.C. § 794a(a)(2) (adopting remedies under Civil Rights Act Title VI, 42 U.S.C. §§ 2000d–2000d-7).

provisions.[262] In an action brought by HUD, an administrative law judge may award damages or equitable relief.[263] The judge also may assess civil penalties of up to $10,000.[264] Reasonable attorney fees also may be awarded to a prevailing party, except where the United States is the prevailing party.[265]

In a private-party action, courts may award punitive damages, actual damages, equitable relief (for example, a restraining order or an injunction), or other appropriate relief.[266] In some instances, prevailing parties may be able to recover reasonable legal costs and fees.[267]

---

262. 42 U.S.C. §§ 3614(a)-(b); 42 U.S.C.(a)(1)(A)(i); 42 U.S.C. § 3602(i).

263. HUD v. Palacios del Rio, HUDALJ 08-046-FH (Oct. 24, 2008); HUD v. Twinbrooke Village Apartments, HUDALJ Nos. 02-00-0256-8, 02-00-0257-8, 02-00-0258-8 (11/09/2001).

264. 42 U.S.C. § 3612(g).

265. 42 U.S.C. § 3612(p).

266. 42 U.S.C. § 3613(c).

267. 42 U.S.C. § 3613(c)(2).

12

ADA Title III

This chapter addresses a couple more points about Title III of the Americans with Disabilities Act (ADA). The information in this chapter is in addition to the information provided elsewhere in the book. Title III applies to private entities, and it precludes discrimination based on disability in the provision of goods, services, facilities, privileges, advantages, or accommodations by any place owning, leasing, or operating a place of public accommodation.[268] Places of public accommodation are places that are not government-owned or government-operated as publicly operated facilities.[269] A partial list of places of public accommodation includes hotels, restaurants, auditoriums, shopping malls, concert halls, retail centers, and banks.[270] Private clubs

---

268. 42 U.S.C. § 12181(7).
269. *Id.*
270. MALLOY, *supra* note 1, at 117.

are not covered under Title III of the ADA unless the private club is open to nonmembers.

Under limited circumstances, single-family homes are covered under Title III of the ADA, even though they are not covered under Title II of the ADA. An example of when a single-family home is covered under Title III of the ADA is a business that operates out of a home.[271] In the case of a home office or a home-based business, the home should be ADA-compliant with respect to an entrance and in the parts of the home where the public is welcome in relation to the business.

While Title III applies to private places of public accommodation, there is an exception for religious organizations and entities that are controlled by religious organizations.[272] The preamble to Title III provides:

> [T]he ADA's exemption of religious organizations and religious entities controlled by religious organizations is very broad, encompassing a wide variety of situations. Religious organizations and entities controlled by religious organizations have no obligations under the ADA. Even when a religious organization carries out activities that would otherwise make it a public accommodation, the religious organization is exempt from ADA coverage. Thus, if a church itself operates . . . a private school, or a diocesan school system, the operations of the . . . school or schools would not be subject to the ADA or [the Title III regulations]. The religious entity would not lose its exemption merely because the services provided

---

271. 28 C.F.R. § 36.207.
272. 42 U.S.C. § 12187.

were open to the general public. The test is whether the church or other religious organization operates the public accommodation, not which individuals receive the public accommodation's services.[273]

But note that if a religious entity receives federal funds, it is subject to Section 504 of the Rehabilitation Act (RHA).[274]

With respect to places of public accommodation and facilities that are subject to Title III, there often is confusion about the requirement to make existing structures accessible. Some property owners may believe that older buildings and facilities that fail to meet current accessible design standards are "grandfathered in" if they are not accessible to people with disabilities. Such a belief is only partially correct and is subject to qualification. The ADA does require the removal of barriers to accessibility in older buildings.[275] Title III also specifically states that for public accommodations, "discrimination includes failure to remove architectural barriers . . . in existing facilities unless it can be shown that removing a barrier is not 'readily achievable' or accommodations cannot be provided through other means."[276]

The Department of Justice (DOJ) regulations for Title III of the ADA are called the 2010 ADA Standards for Accessible Design (*Standards*).[277] These Standards "set minimum requirements . . . for newly designed and constructed, or altered, state and local

---

273. *See* 56 Fed. Reg. 35,554 (July 26, 1991); U.S. Dep't of Justice, ADA Title III Technical Assistance Manual SIII-1.5200 (1992).

274. 29 U.S.C. § 794 (2006).

275. 42 U.S.C. § 12182 (2010).

276. *Id.*

277. U.S. Dep't of Justice, 2010 ADA Standards for Accessible Design, *supra* note 191.

government facilities, public accommodations, and commercial facilities to be "readily accessible to and usable by individuals with disabilities."[278] The Standards incorporate the requirements of 28 C.F.R. 35.151, 28 C.F.R. part 36, Subpart D, and the 2004 United States Access Board (USAB) ADA Accessibility Guidelines (ADAAG).[279] Under the regulations, all newly designed and newly constructed buildings and facilities, and altered portions of existing buildings and facilities, must comply with the ADAAG and be accessible to the "fullest extent possible."[280] The determination of *fullest extent possible* requires accessibility, except when doing so would be "structurally impracticable."[281] The determination of feasibility is not a cost and benefit analysis because the regulations require compliance even if the cost is high.[282]

Importantly, Title III regulations have a safe-harbor provision, which states that elements of covered structures and facilities built or altered before March 15, 2012, that complied with the 1991 Standards for Accessible Design *do not* need to be changed to satisfy the newer 2010 Standards.[283] On the other hand, if an element of a structure or facility already in existence did not comply with the 1991 Standards for Accessible Design prior to March 15, 2012, this element must be modified to meet the newer 2010 Standards to the extent that the modification is readily achievable.[284]

---

278. *Id.*

279. *Id.*

280. *Id.*

281. *Id.* 28 C.F.R. § 35.151.

282. *See generally* De la Rosa v. 597 Broadway Dev. Corp., 2015 WL 7351540 (S.D.N.Y. Aug. 5, 2015), report and recommendation adopted in part, 2015 WL 7308661 (S.D.N.Y. Nov. 19, 2015).

283. 28 C.F.R. § 36.304.

284. *Id.*

The *readily achievable* standard applies to requirements to make modifications to existing buildings and facilities.[285] The readily achievable standard has several criteria and the determination of readily achievable is fact-specific. A change is readily achievable if it is easy to accomplish and can be done without much difficulty. Factors considered in this determination include: the nature and cost of the action required; the overall financial resources available to the entity asked to make the changes; the impact of the action on the entity's operations; and the entity's ability to take the corrective action (for example, does it have the authority to change a structure or is it just a tenant on a lease?).[286] Likewise, consideration is given to assessing whether the corrective action is permitted under regulations imposed by state and local government.

In determining whether an action is readily achievable, the plaintiff has the initial burden of making a prima facie case that a corrective action is readily achievable.[287] If a prima facie case is presented, the burden shifts to the defendant. The defendant has the ultimate burden of demonstrating that the action is not readily achievable. In each instance, evidence might include engineering and architectural reports, cost estimates, financial data, and an assessment of the ability of the defendant to legally take the actions needed to address the accessibility problem. Legality issues may involve such things as assessing lease restrictions or zoning regulations that prevent the corrective action unless they are modified. For example, a restaurant in a shopping center may lack an adequate number of handicap parking spaces,

---

285. *Id.*
286. Hubbard v. Rite Aid Corp., 433 F. Supp. 2d 1150, 1168 (S.D. Cal. 2006).
287. *Id.* at 1159.

but the owners of the restaurant may be unable to correct the problem on their own if the parking lot is owned and controlled by the owner of the shopping center.[288]

It is important to remember that the defense that something is not readily achievable applies only in particular circumstances and when addressing existing buildings and facilities. In all cases of new construction and alterations, compliance with accessibility standards must be met to the fullest extent possible. In these cases, the only defense against this level of compliance is structural impracticability. A high cost to comply is not determinate in the evaluation of structural impracticability.

Considering remedies, a different set of remedies are available under Title II of the ADA than under Title III. The only remedies available under Title III are injunctive relief and attorney fees.[289] When the DOJ brings a cause of action for violating Title III, the court may charge a fine of up to $100,000. No punitive damages are available under Title III.[290]

---

288. *Id.*
289. 42 U.S.C. § 12188; 28 C.F.R. § 36.501.
290. 42 U.S.C. § 12188.

13

Special Provisions and Issues for Housing

In this chapter, we look at special provisions and issues for housing as they relate to the three primary regulatory Acts in federal disability law.

SINGLE-FAMILY HOUSING

Privately owned, single-family, detached homes have the least amount of regulation in terms of the Americans with Disabilities Act (ADA), Section 504 of the Rehabilitative Act (RHA), and the Fair Housing Act (FHA).[291] Generally, design guidelines are limited, but the FHA does apply to housing sales and rentals. In terms of design, there are two common reference points: *universal design* and *visitability*. Universal design seeks to make

---

291. MALLOY, *supra* note 1, at 113; 42 U.S.C. § 3603.

a building universally accessible to the fullest extent possible. It includes entranceways, hallways, access to cabinets, light switches, sinks, showers and bathtubs, and the like. The idea of visitability is that a building or home may not meet all of the requirements of universal design throughout the entire structure, but it is generally accessible enough to be easily and safely visited by a person with a disability, perhaps by a person who is using a wheelchair. This means that the entranceway and the primary social areas of the structure should be accessible, and there should be at least a half-bath that is accessible to visitors.

MULTI-FAMILY HOUSING

The FHA requires "all new multi-family housing to meet specific inclusive design standards, including guidelines for common areas, entranceways, hallways, light switches, grab bars, space to accommodate use of a wheelchair, and other design elements." [292] Design and construction requirements are issued both by the Department of Housing and Urban Development (HUD) and the Department of Justice (DOJ). Any failure to make multi-family housing compliant with these standards is a violation of the FHA.

A multi-family dwelling is defined as "(A) buildings consisting of four or more units if such buildings have one or more elevators; and (B) ground floor units in other buildings consisting of four or more units." [293]

---

292. MALLOY, *supra* note 1, at 114; U.S. DEP'T OF HOUS. & URBAN DEV. and U.S. DEP'T OF JUSTICE, ACCESSIBILITY (DESIGN AND CONSTRUCTION) REQUIREMENTS FOR COVERED MULTIFAMILY DWELLINGS UNDER THE FAIR HOUSING ACT (2013), *supra* note 31.
293. 42 U.S.C. § 3604(f)(7).

PRIVATE VS. PUBLIC HOUSING

HUD enforces Title II of the ADA when it relates to state and local public housing, housing assistance, and housing referrals.[294]

Under HUD regulations, "five percent of qualifying public housing units must be fully accessible in terms of universal design."[295]

CONDOMINIUMS, SUBDIVISIONS, AND COOPERATIVE HOUSING

A "covered multi-family dwelling" under the FHA has design and construction requirements and may include condominiums, cooperatives, apartment buildings, vacation and timeshare units, assisted living facilities, continuing care facilities, nursing homes, public housing developments, housing projects funded with federal funds, transitional housing, single room occupancy

---

294. MALLOY, *supra* note 1, at 116; 42 U.S.C. §§ 12131-12161 (2009).

295. MALLOY, *supra* note 1, at 118. There is a standard of 5% or a minimum of one dwelling unit that must meet mobility impairment regulations for all projects that receive federal financial assistance, including: Section 202/811 capital advances, Section 8 project-based assistance, newly constructed public housing projects, or public housing projects undergoing rehabilitation financed by Comprehensive Improvement Assistance Program (CIAP) funds; *see* U.S. DEP'T OF HOUS. & URBAN DEV., MARK-TO-MARKET PROGRAM OPERATING PROCEDURES GUIDE, app. 1 (attachment B) (DOC 19479.PDF0) (2004), https://www.hud.gov/sites/documents/DOC_19479.PDF and the link to the entire Mark-to-Market procedures is https://www.hud.gov/program_offices/housing/mfh/presrv/presmfh /opglinks. The appendix also references, for further definitions, "New Construction (24 C.F.R. § 8.23(b))," "Substantial Alteration (24 C.F.R. § 8.23(a))," and "Other Alterations/Clarifications (24 C.F.R. § 8.23(b))." *Id.* at B-2. Guidelines for meeting mobility impaired regulations also are outlined and are similar to what one might expect from a form of universal design. *Id.* at B-3; *See generally* U.S. DEP'T OF HOUS. & URBAN DEV., ACCESSIBILITY REQUIREMENTS FOR BUILDINGS, https://www.hud.gov/program_offices/fair_housing_equal_opp/disabilities /accessibilityR (last visited Feb. 4, 2020).

units, shelters designed as residences for homeless persons, dormitories, hospices, and extended stay or residential hotels.[296]

A single-family home may be covered under the FHA as a condominium if it is in a building of four or more units.[297]

The ADA also is relevant in the creation of new condominiums and cooperatives because it provides design and construction guidelines for those building types. Common elements of a condominium need to be accessible under the FHA.[298] Furthermore, while the cooperative board of a condominium retains an absolute right of approval, the board is not allowed to deny the approval of an applicant because of the applicant's disability.

---

296. U.S. Dep't of Hous. & Urban Dev. and U.S. Dep't of Justice, Accessibility (Design and Construction) Requirements for Covered Multifamily Dwellings under the Fair Housing Act (2013), *supra* note 31.

297. Malloy, *supra* note 1, at 114; 24 C.F.R. § 100.25(d) ex. 1 (2008).

298. United States v. Edward Rose & Sons, 384 F.3d 258, 263 (6th Cir. 2004).

14

Historic Districts and Historic Preservation

Our disability laws include special provisions related to historic buildings and districts. In general, the accessibility requirements apply to historic buildings, subject to special considerations.[299] First, to be considered historic, a building or district must be designated as historic by the federal, state, or local government. It is not a historic building or district simply because it is old or because some people think of it that way. Historic designation requires a review and a determination of the features and qualities of the property that make it of historical significance. Existing buildings that were in use prior to March 13, 1991, do

---

299. *See generally* 28 C.F.R. § 36.304, 28 C.F.R. § 405; ADAAG, *supra* note 186, at § 4.1.7; *and* U.S. Dep't of Justice, ADA Title III Technical Assistance Manual, *supra* note 277, at § III-4.4200: " . . . [b]arrier removal would not be considered 'readily achievable' if it would threaten or destroy the historic significance of a building or facility that is . . . designated as historic under State or local law."

not come within the current disability design and construction requirements. Alterations of buildings and facilities made after this date must be done in a way that meets the design requirements to the *maximum extent feasible*. Modifications to the accessibility guidelines are available for historic buildings and properties, but these modifications still require accessibility. The focus generally is on accessible pathways and entrances to the building and an accessible bathroom that has at least one accessible toilet and sink. Special consideration must be given to the regulation of land use when a historic building or structure is involved. The goal is to blend considerations of accessibility with preservation of the features and qualities that give the building its historical significance.

In dealing with historic structures and facilities, often there are stairways, narrow doorways, and other barriers to entry and access to consider. This is because earlier standards of construction did not focus on accessibility in the same way as required by contemporary disability laws.

When a challenge of lack of accessibility is made and the issue is not one of building a new facility or altering a current one, barrier removal is required only when it is readily achievable. Barrier removal is readily achievable when it is "easily accomplishable and able to be carried out without much difficulty or expense." Barrier removal in an existing facility is not readily achievable if, for a property or building that is officially designated as historical, barrier removal would threaten or destroy the historic significance of the property or building. An alteration of an existing structure, as might be the case with remodeling, requires a more stringent standard. This standard is one of making the facility accessible to the maximum extent feasible. With a historic property, the preservation of its historic significance is again considered. New facilities must comply with current guidelines under the ADA. Thus, if one were adding a new museum store near the historic property, this new building would need to be compliant under current standards of accessibility.

A plaintiff generally must make a plausible claim of lack of accessibility, but the defendant generally has the burden of showing that the removal of a barrier from an existing structure is not readily achievable, including establishing the threat posed to the historical significance of the structure or facility.[300]

---

300. Molski v. Foley Estates Vineyard & Winery, LLC, 531 F.3d. 1043 (9th Cir. 2008).

15

Public Entity: Responsible Employee and Grievance Procedures

If you deal with local government planning and zoning, you need to know how it intersects with disability law. In addition, if you represent a public entity, you need to make sure that the entity complies with the regulations that require public entities that employ 50 or more persons to designate a person who is responsible for accessibility, and to adopt and publish grievance procedures. The requirements are found in 28 Code of Federal Regulations (C.F.R.) § 35-107:

28 C.F.R. § 35.107 Designation of responsible employee and adoption of grievance procedures.

(a) Designation of responsible employee. A public entity that employs 50 or more persons shall designate at least one employee to coordinate its efforts to comply with and carry out its responsibilities under this part, including any investigation of any complaint communicated to it alleging its noncompliance with this part or alleging any actions that would be prohibited by this part. The public entity shall make available to all interested individuals the name, office address, and telephone number of the employee or employees designated pursuant to this paragraph.

(b) Complaint procedure. A public entity that employs 50 or more persons shall adopt and publish grievance procedures providing for prompt and equitable resolution of complaints alleging any action that would be prohibited by this part.

Conclusion

Our various disability laws contain many detailed requirements. This book has identified and discussed key provisions of these laws and focused on the ways they most directly impact the work of lawyers in the areas of property, land use, and zoning. These are all areas relevant to local government law. The following chart summarizes some of the primary areas of concern. This summary is in addition to standard lawyering issues related to determining whether a person is covered by the disability laws; identifying which of the acts—the Americans with Disabilities Act (ADA), the Rehabilitation Act (RHA), or the Fair Housing Act (FHA)—the matter falls under; and addressing such issues as standing to bring a case. Likewise, there are legal concerns regarding the definition and classification of such terms and activities as new construction and alterations; facilities; reasonable accommodations and reasonable modifications; programs, services, and activities of local government; structural impracticability; terms like maximum extent possible and readily achievable; service animals; and emotional support animals. All of these are legal issues that are fundamental to matters of accessibility, and all have little to do with matters of design.[301]

---

301. For additional information and resources, *see* https://landuselawanddisability.syr.edu/.

Summary Chart

Subject Area	Concern
Person Protected	*Disability* means having a) a physical or mental impairment that substantially limits one or more major life activities; b) a record of such an impairment; or c) being regarded as having such an impairment. Persons with a disability and some third parties have standing.
New Construction and Alterations	Must be accessible to the maximum extent possible. The only defense to lack of accessibility is "structural impracticability." High cost is not a determinate factor in this defense.
Land Regulations, Zoning, and Lease Restrictions	Enforcement is subject to exceptions because a person with a disability is entitled to a "reasonable accommodation/modification." Determining reasonableness involves a three-factor test: (1) "reasonableness" using a cost and benefit analysis; (2) "necessity" using a "but for" test; and (3) determining that granting the accommodation/modification will not fundamentally alter the program, service, or activity in question.
Programs, Services, and Activities	Must be accessible to people with disabilities. Includes planning and zoning. Defenses include demonstrating that a requested accommodation/modification imposes an "undue administrative or financial burden" on the defendant. Costs are considered.
Rehabilitation and Updating (including historic preservation)	Based on year of construction; older buildings, structures, and facilities are subject to the disability laws. They must be brought up to current accessibility standards to the extent that doing so is "readily achievable."
Animals	Service animals under the ADA specifically include dogs and miniature horses. Service animals need to be trained to do work or perform tasks. Service animals are not pets. If a service animal meets the definition, is housebroken, and is under the control of the owner, it must be permitted to go wherever the person with a disability can go. Under the FHA and RHA, service

animals include emotional support animals; these may be pets. An emotional support animal can be any kind of animal. Subject to a reasonable accommodation/modification determination, emotional support animals may go wherever the public is permitted.

Discrimination

There are multiple ways to demonstrate discrimination against people with a disability. Planning and zoning codes must be careful not to treat uses related to disability differently from other similar type uses. Failure to make facilities, programs, services, and activities accessible to people with a disability is discrimination. More specifically, discrimination can be demonstrated by three methods: (1) disparate treatment; (2) disparate impact; and (3) failure to provide a reasonable accommodation/modification when requested.

Table of Cases

Index